A JOHN CATT PUBLICATION

How to avoid them and h

TOXIC SCHOOLS

Dr Helen Woodley
with Ross Morrison McGill

First Published 2018

by John Catt Educational Ltd,
15 Riduna Park, Station Road
Melton, Woodbridge IP12 1QT

Tel: +44 (0) 1394 389850 Fax: +44 (0) 1394 386893
Email: enquiries@johncatt.com
Website: www.johncatt.com

ISBN: 978 1 911382 98 0

Set and designed by John Catt Educational Limited

Reviews

This is an extremely important and timely read for anyone in education wishing to better understand the characteristics and consequences of toxic school cultures. By shining a light on poor practice through the use of fictionalised narratives, this book also raises questions about how school leaders can look after their teachers and hopefully prevent so many from leaving the profession.

Daryn Egan-Simon
Teacher trainer, PhD researcher and co-founder of BrewEd

A welcome and timely addition to the burgeoning literature of school staff wellbeing. At its heart is a collection of authentic teacher stories, viewed through the lens of Dr Woodley's analysis of toxic schools. The marriage of academic rigour with practical advice, built upon research, makes this book an important contribution to the wider wellbeing debate.

Sam Collins
Teacher and founder of Schoolwell

Toxic Schools takes what others might wish to hide away and brings it centre stage. It shines a bright light on how some schools create and sustain cultures that damage individual teachers and the profession as a whole. It is a call-out which we all need to hear. And it is also a call to arms. Reading this book, reflecting on its content and discussing the insights it helps us to generate offers us a language and a conceptual framework for change. Schools can change for the better from the inside out, and this book might be a major contribution to creating that change.

Professor Rachel Lofthouse
Professor of Teacher Education, founder of CollectivED

In the current educational climate – in which the teacher crisis, far from alleviating, is getting even worse – this book is not just important but essential reading for policy-makers and school leaders. Many of the stories are truly horrific. However, it's important to note that the book is written from a place of love, loyalty and the fierce, righteous and justified rage at those who make 'what can already feel like a challenging job into one which can feel like a Herculean task'. Helen's background as an academic researcher gives the book real clout and credibility.

Dr Emma Kell
Teacher, Doctor of Education, author

This book provides a unique insight into teachers' personal experiences in toxic schools, and offers some solutions to the issues.

Toxic cultures in schools are born of putting performance before teachers. As a result, this leads to teachers being stressed out and talented teachers leaving to pursue greener pastures.

Helen's and Ross's observations highlight the future of schools: success will not be in league tables but in how well a school values health and wellbeing.

Mark Martin
Teacher and founder of Urban Teacher

Toxic Schools reminds us of the importance and value of listening to each individual teacher's voice. It's a thought-provoking body of work and a must-read for all us senior leaders who should constantly be striving to explore meaningful school self-evaluation. Are we really who we think we are? *Toxic Schools* reminds us all of the importance of how Senior Leadership Teams communicate, our influence on other individuals and the powerful effect that our words may have.

Andria Zafirakou
Global Teacher Prize Winner 2018

Toxic Schools shines a powerful light on an issue that should concern everyone in education. Through a series of startlingly vivid portraits of life working in toxic schools, this book brings into sharp focus the critical importance of valuing and celebrating the right leadership behaviours. This is a thought-provoking read about the importance of people and relationships.

We cannot truly consider ourselves a high-functioning profession if we treat staff working in schools as renewable resources to be used and replaced. *Toxic Schools* will be a mirror in which teachers and leaders alike can reflect on their own experiences, whilst it provides useful and pragmatic suggestions to help take control in toxic environments.

Nick Brook
Deputy General Secretary, NAHT

Contents

Introduction – Voices from inside toxic schools

This book does not aim to be a textbook for how to prevent a school becoming toxic, nor is it a step-by-step self-help guide for coping in one. Instead, it is about hearing the authentic voices of teachers who have worked in toxic settings, understanding the common threads of their experiences, seeing how these may overlap with your own experiences, and trying to forge a way forward. It is written both from my experience of being a classroom teacher who has had her own experiences of working in toxic settings and from the point of view of an academic researcher with an interest in some of the key themes that will be discussed.

Toxic work environments are challenging places to be in. They are negative places for all the staff who work there, even if they only cause obvious effects to a few staff. Toxic schools can turn confident and able teachers into ones who doubt their ability and may only seek to leave the profession. Equally, they can impact upon leaders, both established and aspiring, in the same way. The longer you work within a toxic school, the more likely it is for you to begin to accept it and to find your own values and philosophy slowly diminish and change into something else; you become the teacher you never wanted to be and cannot pinpoint where it all unravelled. This doesn't have to be the case. By recognising what toxic schools are, understanding how they affect teachers, and striving to create environments which are not toxic, we can gradually reduce the impact they have on the education system.

In this book several key concepts are discussed, including teacher voice, fictionalised narratives and ethnography. These underpin the majority of the content; and although they are discussed at length in key areas, they are frequent themes which pop up throughout the chapters. Reference is made to significant research in these areas and lists of suggested further reading is included at the end of each chapter.

Agreeing upon what we mean by 'teacher voice' is tricky as there are multiple definitions. Some may understand it in terms of having a voice at a national level within policies or politics; some may perceive it as their right to criticise those in governance and leadership of them; yet others may see it as having a voice within their specific area of expertise. Rather than trying to simplify teacher voice and risk losing some of the richness it contains, we should instead accept its complexity. Over the last 20 years, the importance of student voice in education has grown but the relevance of teacher voice has been gradually undermined. The role of the teacher is often less about a professional dialogue with school leaders on the ethos and culture of a school and more about staff performing their allotted duties within the classroom; teachers are often kept within a well defined box. Chapter 11 of this book aims to show how teacher voice can be used as an important tool for combating toxic school environments.

This book will also show how fictionalised narratives can be used as a tool for teachers to share their authentic voices whilst remaining within the bounds of their professional duties. Fictionalised narratives, also known as ethnographic fiction, can be understood by comparing them to historical novels. While these are works of fiction with the author responsible for imagining the dialogue and emotions of the characters, they also share knowledge and information about a specific period of history; they are about events that did happen, yet they are presented in a way imagined by the author. In a similar way, fictionalised narratives aim to show the *truth* of what people say or do yet are also *untrue* at the same time. We will discuss their use in education further in chapter 3.

Fictionalised research can seek to overcome some of the professional boundaries teachers face and further engage them in having a voice in education and educational research.

Ethnography is an important theme for this book because it is based upon the premise that teachers are talking, blogging or writing about their lived experiences of a specific social community: schools. The importance of hearing voices from within the classroom is crucial for many reasons. Teachers are best placed to be writing and sharing details about their professional lives. Whilst there is a definite place for research in schools by 'outsiders', it is those within the classroom who have the real window to the world of education. Their voices are the ones we need to hear. Chapter 11 looks at how teachers can use the principles of ethnography to change some of the accepted narratives about working in challenging school environments.

Helen Woodley

Most teachers and school leaders will be able to describe to you 'when' and 'why' they have worked in a challenging school, but not many people will be able to explain how they survived (assuming they did). Taking the context of 'challenging schools' a little further, do you know of any teachers who could share examples of working and surviving in a toxic school? A school which has a poisonous working culture where numbers – grades, cash or both – are the main drivers to its (apparent) success.

Not everyone has worked in a toxic school, but we may be familiar with situations at work when relationships with our peers have become poisoned and incurable.

Despite people working in our schools to educate the next generation of pupils to grow up with strong morals and collective values and to make positive contributions to society, why do some people inside our education system believe that poisonous behaviour is the way forward? And despite having a recruitment and retention crisis on our hands, we have people inside the system driving good teachers away from our schools!

In Helen's book, she shares her doctoral research and case studies from teachers who have been on the receiving end of toxic behaviours. There's a good chance you may recognise the findings of this research from your own experience or from observations of colleagues who have shown toxic behaviours. You may have worked in a toxic culture or simply want to understand what toxic schools are, why they develop and how we can alleviate toxicity from our schools.

You may even be a person who has displayed toxic behaviours or knows someone who does. Whatever it is, this book is an important step forward in educational research and Helen's contribution in this field is significant.

Ross Morrison McGill

Reflections

Chapter 1 - Identifying a toxic school

Why the interest in toxic schools?

My interest in toxic schools grew out of my doctoral thesis, which had a focus on teacher voice. I had not intended to focus on this, but over the course of my research, my interest in teacher voice grew with my own awareness that my own voice was often unheard outside of the team I worked with. I was fortunate that I ended up working in a setting that encouraged teacher voice, that allowed staff professional autonomy, and that supported us with our aspirations. I was able to reflect back upon other experiences in my career and see how potentially damaging they had been due to a lack of these features. I began to record my thoughts and feelings in a journal and found that this self-writing was beneficial. As Tim O'Brien suggests in his book *Inner Story*, understanding the private stories which we tell ourselves can give us a greater understanding of how we exist in the world around us (O'Brien, 2015). From these separate stories in my journal, I began to write a more detailed account of my own experiences using a form of writing called autoethnography, which will be discussed in greater detail in chapter 3. However, for a definition, it is a form of writing where the author uses self-reflection to write themselves into the social world (Denshire, 2014). Throughout this book, autoethnographical writing is used because the story told has some relevance to the issue being discussed. This is largely due to the fact that, for my own autoethnographical writing, the social world I inhabit is one of schools and education.

One personal autoethnographic narrative stands out. It occurred at a time in my life that I was suffering from an immense personal crisis:

> I was a relatively young teacher working in an all-age special school. I was young, enthusiastic, and troubled by my life outside of school. It was the build up to Christmas and, in school, a time of immense joy, continuous fun, and the inevitable school production. My class were involved in the performance and the frequency of rehearsals had grown as the end of term drew near. With the performance a matter of days away, the school was gathered in the hall to have a final run through. My hard work was over: I had taught the class the songs with the accompanying Makaton signs and we had hastily painted the large pieces of cardboard which were due to become the stable scene. Yet, in my private life, I was coping with the after effects of my partner having an affair. I had told key staff at school (including my line manager) about my situation and was very much in the mindset that I just needed to get through until the end of term, which was only a matter of weeks away. I had managed to cope with the performance of teaching in the classroom but the endless rehearsals for the play were taking their toll. On this particular afternoon, I was stood in the dark at the back of the hall as a mere spectator whilst the staff in charge of the production directed the pupils around the stage. Having been so intensely involved before, I was glad of the chance to take a step back and revel in the enchantment of my class performing on stage. Initially the thrill of seeing them sing and sign was wonderful. The smiles on their faces were genuine and all of the stresses of the past weeks of practising had gone. However, in those few private moments alone at the back of the hall, my guard slipped: the smile dropped and a few tears

escaped down my face. The joy of watching my class had been like an inverted reflection of my own life and had highlighted how sad and grey it felt.

Unbeknown to me, my line manager – let's call her Evie – had moved close to me in the hall. We had not got on for several years, largely because I had not joined the group of teachers who swarmed around her as so any others had before. It hadn't been that I disliked her – in fact, I had initially thought her to be welcoming and vivacious – but I quickly realised that she was quite insecure and used the attention of other teachers to boost her confidence. I had decided that I would rather not fall into that role so I had been polite but kept my own counsel. This had only served to frustrate her, and over the months we had grown further and further apart. As the lights were turned on in the hall, she saw my tear-stained face. Rather than offering a word of consolation or a hug, she said with menace, 'Get a smile on your face; it's nearly bloody Christmas. Look happy.'

That single comment almost ended my teaching career as I suddenly realised how undervalued and unsupported I was. I looked at my school with fresh eyes and saw the exhaustion, stress, and sadness in many of the faces around me. Over the next few months I began to hear the stories of other staff around me who had fallen victim to the caustic wit and criticisms which dripped from Evie's mouth. Those who had either not been selected to join Evie's group – or had actively decided to avoid it – had made their classrooms their places of sanctuary. As I began to spend more and more time with them, I realised that I could not remain in the school for much longer. I knew that whilst Evie remained in a position of leadership and influence, things were not going to change. Plus the divisions between the staff were too entrenched and I could not see how they would ever be bridged. It was my first permanent contract and the prospect of walking away was awful as much as it felt necessary. Thankfully, I decided to give education another chance and moved to a school which I loved, but I could have so easily have left the professional altogether.

This self-reflection through autoethnography gave me an interest in the hidden lives of other teachers I met. It was only during my final year of writing my thesis that I rediscovered Twitter and was astounded at the snippets of lives I read there, often from teachers who were struggling in their professional worlds. They were honest and open and had found some release in having their voices heard on social media, even if they were not heard in their schools. Many of them were trying hard to keep their professional pain away from tainting their families or home lives. I realised that there were many teachers who spent their days feeling isolated and unheard. Often they were working within schools where the school culture and leadership were preventing teachers from having a voice. I realised how fortunate I was to be able to work with a team with whom I could share the whole of myself and find support, encouragement, and a cup of coffee, even if I felt silenced in other areas of my professional life.

It struck me that some of the teachers on Twitter had never been in a position to have their voices heard at all – not within their teams or departments, and sometimes not within their own classrooms. I began to chat with them, trying to link them with people that I knew could help or simply providing a space for them to offload. Some of these relationships developed to such a degree that they wanted to have the opportunity to tell their full stories. The more time I spent talking with them, the more I was able to see common threads which reappeared time and time again across a variety of settings, age ranges, and career stages. These threads became the basis for the concept of this book.

I am indebted to these professionals for their honesty, their openness and their desire to help others either in the same situation or those leading a school which has a toxic culture.

In this opening chapter from Helen, you will read how using an autoethnographic process evolved into this book, stemming from a moment in school which became 'an inverted reflection' of her own life. This private moment almost ended her teaching career.

Caustic wit, sarcasm and critique became the norm at work until social media – how we live and work online – started to offer opportunities for Helen to observe, to connect and discover common threads with other teachers all around the world.

In my 25 years teaching in schools, I've never worked in a toxic school; but I have found myself in toxic situations several times – key moments that make an impression on your long-term memory throughout your career. Whether this makes for a toxic school will be defined throughout this book; but in my case, these circumstances led to me leaving a job I loved – twice.

Characteristics of a toxic school

Many teachers, myself included, have come home from work and ranted and moaned about where we work and who we work with. This letting-off of steam is normal behaviour and a way of coping with the low-level stress and frustrations that we all feel; it is not necessarily an indication that we work within a toxic school. So, what is? How do we know that we have tipped over the edge and we are experiencing something that can affect our mental and physical health? When should we start to be concerned?

There is no blueprint for what a toxic school is; they can be high-achieving, low-achieving, in challenging socio-economic areas, in affluent areas, in cities, or in the countryside. Many teachers will work in such a school during their careers or hear anecdotes about experiences colleagues have had. Largely they are not discussed or talked about by staff working within them due to the effect they have on teacher self-esteem or due to staff fear of being seen as a whistleblower on practice. As a profession, we are not encouraged to share our voice on our workplaces. After all, Part Two of the *Teachers' Standards* requires:

> 'Teachers must have proper and professional regard for the ethos, policies and practices of the school in which they teach, and maintain high standards in their own attendance and punctuality.' (Department for Education, 2011)

Whilst there are teachers who are fully aware that their workplace is toxic, many teachers may not even realise they are working in such an environment, instead internalising any difficulties they face and presuming that they are weak, are missing something obvious to everyone else, or are simply not a very good teacher. It is only when they move on, either to a new school or a new profession, that they are able to reflect on their experiences and realise that it was their school that was to blame, not themselves. Five such teachers (some now *former* teachers) will share their experiences of working in toxic schools in part 2 of this book.

If it is so hard to define what a toxic school is, how can we seek to identify one? Imagine your ideal school setting. A positive school culture is one that staff and learners enjoy being in and actively want to work in because they value the school and feel valued in return. Positive schools promote and support pupils to pursue high academic standards. Leadership is inclusive and supportive, and cooperation between staff and other stakeholders helps to create a setting where pupils and staff can succeed. In a positive school culture, a caring atmosphere exists, and teachers have a sense of responsibility for their pupils as leaders do for their staff. A positive school is simply where, the majority of the time, staff are motivated, pupils encouraged and leaders approach their role with a high level of emotional intelligence.

Toxic schools are the direct opposite. Toxic schools are filled with teachers who are unhappy with their jobs. Both teachers and pupils are not academically motivated; where pupils do academically succeed it is largely due to external factors and not due to the provision the school offers. Schools with a toxic culture don't have a clear sense of purpose and their ethos is not clearly defined. A toxic school often discourages collaboration and frequently experiences hostility between staff, pupils and leaders. The key factor of a toxic school is this: leadership is, at some level, aware and yet does not actively seek to develop the school culture to become more positive, either because they are unwilling or unable.

Every teacher's experience within a toxic school is unique due to the individuals involved and their particular experiences. However, from the narratives shared in part 2, we can identify eight common features which may be experienced in a toxic school setting:

1. High staff turnover

Within the UK education system in 2015, 10% of teachers left the profession (Worth et al., 2015), which equates to around 40,000 people. Yet these figures do not take into account the number of teachers who change schools within an academic year and this information is not available, as records have not been kept. I believe that statistics about the movement of staff from school to school would be crucial in being able to identify possible toxic workplaces.

There may be several reasons why schools experience a high turnover of staff but we shall focus on two which anecdotally appear to be dominant: ethos and socio-economic factors. Firstly, research by Smithers and Robinson (2005) highlighted the fact that teachers were more likely to stay in schools where there was a clearly defined aim and ethos. If you find yourself in a school where you disagree with its aims, you are more likely to leave than if the values mirror your own. We can label such teachers 'idealists' due to their passion to work in an education setting which fits with an education philosophy that is unmet in their current setting (Haberman, 2005). Secondly, there is higher turnover in schools in areas of socio-economic disadvantage (Muijs et al., 2004), something which organisations such as Teach First have tried to address by equipping teachers to work in more challenging settings (Teach First, 2018). Research into why teachers leave these schools indicated that a lack of support is a primary factor (Simon and Johnson, 2015). However, it must be noted that there are schools which are not in areas of socio-economic need that also have a high turnover of staff.

In summary, a school with high turnover is either:

- a situation where teachers leave within their first year of employment, either for career sidesteps or promotion. They are staff that arrive, realise they have ended up in the wrong place, and flee before they become too embedded.
- a school which has a rapid turnover of staff with many changes to the setting every year, often due to staff being poorly supported to fulfil their role.

2. A 'sinking' school

We can call a school 'sinking' when staff are demotivated and unable to change the pattern of behaviour they are in (Stoll and Fink, 1996). Staff have effectively become stuck in a rut and spend each day turning up, going through the motions, and going home. There is also low staff turnover and low morale due to the teachers' lack of value in their own 'professional selves' (Kelchtermans, 1999): if you have come to think of yourself as incapable and not very good at teaching, you are unlikely to apply for a job in a new school where these perceived failings will be easily identified; safer to stay where you are and survive. They may also be staff who feel that they have missed their opportunity to leave (possibly regretting not trying earlier) and now believe that they are institutionalised in their current school.

In summary, a sinking school is one where staff have become emotionally detached, arriving every day because they are contractually obliged to and not because they *want* to; they have a low commitment to their role, and therefore do the bare minimum expected to be kept employed (Haberman, 2005).

3. A 'hothouse' school

This is a school highly controlled by leaders that can be claustrophobic and pressurised (Hargreaves, 1995). This is the sort of school where teachers have to hand in a planning file every Friday, where there is an expectation that displays are triple mounted, and where staff are required to join in with every element of school life. It is a school with a firmly embedded ethos which all new staff subscribe to because everyone else does and you do not want be the person standing out. This pressure can lead to anxiety that you are not doing enough or meeting your full potential (Hargreaves, 2003).

In summary, a hothouse school is one where pressure is applied over a sustained period of time so that it becomes part of the school's culture. Staff are expected to embrace the ethos fully and pressure may come:

- externally from others pointing out your lack of commitment.
- internally from your own anxiety.

4. Repeated restructuring

This term describes a school policy of full or partial restructuring on an annual or bi-annual basis. The initial restructuring may come from an amalgamation, academisation, or a change in leadership. Research informs us that successful restructuring is that which staff are fully involved in through a democratic process (Leech and Fulton, 2008). A school with a successful structure has developed 'relational trust' between leaders, staff, pupils and parents (Bryk and Schneider, 2003); there is collaboration and understanding of the roles and needs of each group.

Repeated restructuring can be an indication that the initial plan has not been achieved and, like a house made of wooden blocks, is redesigned and rebuilt. However, people, unlike wooden blocks, have emotional responses and respond positively or negatively to changes in role, status, and income. If this is then repeated several times, staff can be left unsure about the school culture they are in and feel insecure, assuming that further change may happen. Whilst the need for change might have been initially welcomed or understood, the mismanagement of change can lead to disengagement (Gill, 2002). When each restructuring is further accompanied by other 'reforms' that are never fully embedded into practice, the disengagement can grow.

In summary, a school that repeatedly restructures itself is one where staff experience constant cultural change, often with a lack of engagement in the process.

5. Bureaucratic

This describes a school which is led from the top in a traditional and hierarchical manner; it is the most common organisational structure for both primary and secondary schools (James et al., 2014). The structure is triangular with the head or executive head firmly at the top; they are often viewed as the figurehead. A bureaucratic school has clear rules, clear systems and procedures, and explicit job roles. Teachers are distant from decision-making, with the authority to do this resting in the higher levels; and it can be difficult to break out of the position you are employed in unless you are moving to another set role. Staff can feel happy in such an environment when the school ethos matches their own principles (DiPaola and Tschannen-Moran, 2014) or when they feel that it provides stability (Kean and Piaw, 2017).

Problems arise when the hierarchical and fixed structure doesn't represent the knowledge and needs of those within it. Schools are intricate structures and the simplicity of the hierarchical system often misses nuances and individual needs of those working within it. Some hierarchical systems can also become overly complicated, making them hard to manage. This is especially true in some secondary schools (James et al., 2014).

In summary, bureaucratic schools can have a tendency to be rigid in structure, systems and culture. They can be compared to a large ship at sea: everyone has a set job to do to keep the ship running and it is not easy to slow down or change direction.

6. A teaching culture of 'balkanisation'

This is a school where groups have established within different departments or type of staff; for example, Learning Support Assistants (LSAs) in a distinct group from teachers (Hargreaves, 1994). Originally coined to describe the repeated fragmentation of the Balkan Peninsula, 'balkanisation' has come to be used to describe the breaking-up of a larger entity into smaller units, such as regions of the internet splitting into insular subgroups divided by political interest. This fragmentation leads to each group looking out for their specific needs as a priority, often disregarding the needs or wishes of others. This type of school is often found in secondary schools where there is internal competition for funds or attention from leadership (Rice, 2014). However, I believe that it can be a culture within any school large enough to sustain at least two distinct factions. For example, a large two-form-entry primary school with nursery provision may have an Early Years Foundation Stage (EYFS) group, a KS1 group, KS2 group and possibly a split between teachers and support staff. Balkanisation often leads to conflicts between groups.

In summary, a school experiencing balkanisation is one where many staff end up in distinct groups. There is a lack of movement between the groups as each member of staff generally only has the required attributes for one specific group; movement between groups tends to be informal and dependent on the specifics of individual schools. Leaving the group can lead to social isolation.

7. A teaching culture of 'individualism'

This can be found in a school where each teacher works alone in isolation from everyone else for any of a variety of reasons, including a personal desire to work alone or a culture which has developed individualism as a key principle (Hargreaves, 1994). For some staff, the desire to work alone comes from a fear that collaboration is giving away their knowledge without any reward or payback (Trauth, 1999); there is no motivation to collaborate if you believe that you are the one working whilst your colleague is just coasting thanks to your efforts. Research indicates that this is the default way that teachers work in school unless they are supported to be collaborative (Leonard and Leonard, 2003). Working in an individualist school can be isolating but can also make it hard to progress as a teacher at all due to the lack of support from more experienced colleagues (Williams et al., 2001).

In summary, a culture of individualism is common in many schools, often for large parts of the day. However, this can become problematic when there is no collaboration, either formal or informal, between staff.

8. A 'groupthink' mentality

A school affected by groupthink ignores possible alternatives to its choices and tends to take irrational actions which often dehumanise others (Janis, 1972). The group, whilst working together, is highly dysfunctional (Leithwood et al., 1997). A groupthink school can have good teamwork; however, the lack of criticism within the group serves to reinforce negative actions, meaning the teamwork has negative outcomes (Duke, 2006).

In groupthink schools, an individual's personal beliefs are put to one side – out of anxiety to conform or a desire to be accepted – in order to become part of the group. The group then continues to collectively control the behaviour of every member of the group. Existing outside of a groupthink is isolating; trying to leave the groupthink is challenging.

In summary, a school with a groupthink mentality is one where negative behaviours are reinforced by the collective. Being on the outside of the group is challenging and many change their behaviour in order to fit in.

Making a toxic school

One of these factors alone does not make a toxic school; it is the combination of factors, and the length of time for which they exist, that makes a school toxic. Two or more of these factors lasting for a sustained period of time can lead a school being labelled 'toxic'; and the larger the number of features, the greater the toxicity levels experienced by staff.

Many schools will go through several of these features during their existence and that is perfectly normal as leadership roles change or the social demographic of the local area shifts. The difference with a toxic school is that these factors are persistent and longstanding, often over a significant number of years. They have simply become part of the school culture (an area that will be discussed in greater depth in chapter 2) and are therefore accepted as being normal for working there. This normalisation of toxic factors means that many staff will not be able to recognise their school for what it is – a potential risk to the wellbeing and mental health of those who teach there.

Examples of toxic schools

Iain works in a primary school with a well-known headteacher. The staff turnover is high and the jobs which are advertised are for Main Pay Scale (MPS) teachers only. There is a high number of Newly Qualified Teachers (NQTs) or teachers within the first few years of their career. Although there is a deputy head and key stage assistant heads, the decisions are made by the headteacher, with the SLT responsible for ensuring that staff are informed. Teachers are expected to 'get on with it' and there is little or no collaboration.

- High staff turnover
- Bureaucratic
- Individualist

Sarah works in a large special needs school. The teaching assistants eat in the staffroom and reserve chairs for each other so that there is nowhere for teachers to sit. This means that they eat alone in their classrooms. Sarah is an NQT and is the first new member of staff to join the school in over 7 years. The school has been through several periods of restructuring with many changes to the size of the Senior Leadership Team (SLT).

- Sinking
- Restructuring
- Balkanisation

We must remember...

We must remember what a toxic school is *not*. A school is not toxic simply because one member of staff in unhappy working there. Many teachers experience schools which they dislike and actively try to leave; and the simple fact is that there are schools in which individual staff don't feel happy or professionally challenged. This does not mean that the school itself is toxic. The unique position of a toxic school, as mentioned earlier, is that at some level, leadership *know* that it is one but are unwilling or unable to change it. Toxic schools are those that work against staff as they can target staff working within them (as we shall see in Martyn's story in chapter 8), or allow others within the environment to do so (as Brendan and Jessica experience in chapters 5 and 7 respectively).

Why doesn't every teacher in a toxic school suffer?

The likelihood is that we will all encounter a toxic school at some point in our career either through working in one or hearing about colleagues who do. So, why don't all staff working in one become affected to the same degree? There are several factors which make staff more vulnerable to struggling in a toxic school:

1. External issues

If you are already coping with stressful or challenging situations in your personal life such as a divorce, a new baby, caring for elderly relatives or suffering from a medical issue, your resilience to coping in a toxic school will be lowered. You may also find it harder to seek support due to lack of time or energy to do so. Brendan's story in chapter 5 highlights how this can happen.

2. Personality type

Firstly, some people have a better ability to cope with challenging circumstances. We all know people who seem to deal with everything that gets thrown at them. Secondly, it is also true that some people are naturally more reflective and therefore able to share their concerns at an early stage. Finally, some people are just harder to get along with than others. Who we are impacts upon how we cope. Gwen's and Jessica's stories in chapters 6 and 7 highlight how who we are affects the choices we make when working in a toxic school.

3. Career stage

A third of newly qualified teachers leave within the first five years of teaching (Weale, 2016) and it is therefore reasonable to conclude that a lack of experience of working in a range of settings may leave them more vulnerable to cope within a toxic school if they face one early in their career. Early-career-stage teachers are often focused on getting their teaching 'right' and may not have developed a wider skill set which can support the social and relational nature of schools. The stories of Richard and Jessica in chapters 4 and 7 highlight how more experienced teachers cope compared to those at the start of their career.

4. Toxic schools can change

Just because we find a specific school to be toxic does not mean that it always will be. If a school does not have many toxic features to start with, or goes through a period of immense cultural change, then it can become a different type of environment to work in. This was highlighted to me as, several years after I left a toxic school, I met up with an old colleague who enthusiastically informed me how wonderful my old workplace had become and how much she was enjoying working there.

In the next chapter we will look at how toxic schools are created through school culture and the impact of working in one, both for teachers and learners.

Bibliography

Bryk, A. S. and Schneider, B. (2003) 'Trust in schools: a core resource for school reform', *Educational Leadership* 60 (6) pp. 40–45.

Denshire, S. (2014) 'On auto-ethnography', *Current Sociology* 62 (6) pp. 831–850.

Department for Education (2011) *Teachers' standards*. London: The Stationery Office.

DiPaola, M. and Tschannen-Moran, M. (2014) 'Organizational citizenship behavior in schools and its relationship to school climate', *Journal of School Leadership* 11 (5) pp. 424–447.

Duke, D. L. (2006) What We Know and Don't Know About Improving Low-Performing Schools. *Phi Delta Kappan*. 87, 729-734.

Gill, R. (2003) 'Change management – or change leadership?', *Journal of Change Management* 3 (4) pp. 307–318.

Haberman, M. (2005) 'Teacher burnout in black and white', *The New Educator* 1 (3) pp. 153–175.

Hargreaves, A. (1994) *Changing teachers, changing times: teachers' work and culture in the postmodern age*. New York, NY: Teachers College Press.

Hargreaves, D. (1995) 'School culture, school effectiveness and school improvement', *School effectiveness and School Improvement* 6 (1) pp. 23–46.

Hargreaves, D. (2003) 'Helping practitioners explore their school's culture' in Preedy, M., Glatter, R. and Wise, C. (eds) *Strategic leadership and educational improvement*. London: Paul Chapman Publishing, pp. 109–122.

James, C., Connolly, M., Brammer, S., Fertig, M., James, J. and Jones, J. (2014) 'A comparison of the governing of rimary and secondary schools in England', *School Leadership & Management* 34 (2) pp. 104–119.

Janis, I. L. (1972) *Victims of groupthink: a psychological study of foreign-policy decisions and fiascoes*. Boston, MA: Houghton Mifflin.

Teoh, H. K. and,Chua, Y. P. (2017) 'The effect of school bureaucracy on the relationship between school principal leadership practices and teacher commitment in Malaysia secondary schools', *Educational Leader (Pemimpin Pendidikan)* 5 (1) pp. 37–58.

Kelchtermans, G. (1999) 'Narrative-biographical research on teachers' professional development: exemplifying a methodological research procedure', *Annual meeting of the American Educational Research Assosciation*. Montreal, QC, 19th–23rd April.

Leech, D. and Fulton, C. R. (2008) 'Faculty perceptions of shared decision making and the principal's leadership behaviors in secondary schools in a large urban district', *Education* 128 (4) pp. 630–645.

Leithwood, K., Steinbach, R. and Ryan, S. (1997) 'Leadership and team learning in secondary schools', *School Leadership & Management* 17 (3) pp. 303–326.

Leonard, L. and Leonard, P. (2003) 'The continuing trouble with collaboration: teachers talk', *Current Issues in Education* 6 (15).

Muijs, D., Harris, A., Chapman, C., Stoll, L. and Russ, J. (2004) 'Improving schools in socioeconomically disadvantaged areas – a review of research evidence', *School Effectiveness and School Improvement* 15 (2) pp. 149–175.

O'Brien, T. (2015) *Inner story: understand your mind. Change your world.* Scotts Valley, CA: CreateSpace Independent Publishing Platform.

Rice, S. M. (2014) 'Working to maximise the effectiveness of a staffing mix: what holds more and less effective teachers in a school, and what drives them away?', *Educational Review* 66 (3) pp. 311–329.

Simon, N. S. and Johnson, S. M. (2015) 'Teacher turnover in high-poverty schools: what we know and can do', *Teachers College Record* 117 (3) pp. 1–36.

Smithers, A. and Robinson, P. (2005) *Teacher turnover, wastage and movements between schools.* Department for Education and Skills. London: The Stationery Office.

Stoll, L. & Fink, D. (1996) *Changing our schools: linking school effectiveness and school improvement.* Buckingham: Open University Press.

Teach First (2018) 'Our mission', *Teach First* website. Available at: www.teachfirst.org.uk/our-mission

Trauth, E. M. (1999) 'Who owns my soul? The paradox of pursing organizational knowledge in a work culture of individualism', *ACM SIGCPR conference on computer personnel research.* New Orleans, LA, 8th–10th April. New York, NY: ACM, pp. 159–163.

Weale, S. (2016) 'Almost a third of teachers quit state sector within five years of qualifying', *The Guardian* website. Available at: www.theguardian.com/education/2016/oct/24/almost-third-of-teachers-quit-within-five-years-of-qualifying-figures

Williams, A., Prestage, S. and Bedward, J. (2001) 'Individualism to collaboration: the significance of teacher culture to the induction of newly qualified teachers', *Journal of Education for Teaching* 27 (3) pp. 253–267.

Worth, J., Bamford, S. and Durbin, B. (2015) *Should I stay or should I go? NFER analysis of teachers joining and leaving the profession*. Slough: NFER.

Reflections

Chapter 2 – The creation of toxic schools and the effect on those within them

In this chapter, Helen tackles the difficult topic of 'culture' and how this can be seen (or not) in schools. From the simple day-to-day expectations regarding litter, uniform and rigour in lessons, to the more complex nature of exclusions, curriculum and vision and values, what schools choose to do largely depends on their context.

An indication of a strong school culture is when nothing changes when high-profile visitors or events take place. The workforce carries on as normal.

Creation – school culture

At the most basic level we all have an intrinsic human need to belong and a positive school culture is one where we can have the possibility of experiencing this (Baumeister and Leary, 1995). We can compare this to a negative, or toxic, environment which creates a form of dissonance where the ethics and philosophies of those working in the school are not matched by the wider visible culture (Rosenberg, 1977).

We must remember that 'school culture' is a broad term which encompasses many different ideas. It can be difficult to define but can be explained as 'the way things are done around here' (Stoll and Fink, 1996) and the general feeling which you get for a school from what you see around you. Culture is built from metaphors, customs, rituals, ceremonies, myths, symbols, and stories. In schools we see these many areas including the names in a school house system, stories passed on from pupil to pupil about certain teachers, and the school logo on blazer pockets. It is a mixture of both visible and invisible elements which are uniquely combined within every setting. It includes everything from the type of school building you are working within to the type of pupils your school caters for. The invisible school culture is a truer reflection of the real nature of a school than the visible one because it is the one experienced by those who work there rather than the 'brand' that the school wishes to market.

The visible school culture is the one which a non-member of the community is likely to see on websites, reception areas, and Ofsted banners. It is in the decisions that schools make to display class and staff photos, whether they have awards on the walls, or even if they provide seats for visitors to sit on. Every school now appears to have a mission statement which is broadly publicised on the website and will usually be the first proclamation you see written at the reception. It often uses the words 'inclusive', 'happy', 'proud', and 'inspiring'. This use of mission statements has transferred directly from the branding and marketing of businesses, where research is carried out into the best language to use to convey their ethos and ethics (Chun and Davies, 2001). Within the business sector, the aim is to gain a foothold in a crowded marketplace and develop a brand loyalty that attracts both consumers and investors and portrays a uniqueness to stakeholders. However, there is a danger that the heart and soul of a setting gets lost in a narrow or ill-defined statement, especially if it was not created collectively and bears no relation to the people in the organisation (Fritz, 1996).

Yet do these mission statements actually *mean* anything if they are pulled apart? If we begin to unpick them and question the language used then they can quickly appear to be merely 'happy talk' rather than having any real depth (Rozycki, 2004). For example, take a school which has the following mission statement:

> 'We are an inclusive and happy school where we encourage all children to achieve'

If we begin to ask questions then the use of the mission statement in understanding the invisible and 'real-life' school culture may fall apart. One question raised could be 'If you are inclusive, what is your fixed-term exclusion/permanent exclusion rate?' Over the years, I have worked with many permanently excluded young people whose excluding school's mission statement mentioned 'inclusion'. We could also question the use of the word 'happy' – shouldn't every school provide a happy place for children? So why highlight that your school does in particular? Also, isn't one of the basic functions of a school to encourage achievement? Mission statements do not tell you anything about the invisible culture of a school or what it would be like to work there. Neither do Ofsted banners.

> Schools use Ofsted banners for advertising purposes. Ofsted actively promote on social media how schools should and should not use their logo (for the 'good' and 'outstanding' schools) for copyright reasons as well as celebratory.
>
> In an increasingly online world, what impact does a poster on the street actually have? There is little or no data to capture the number of times someone walks past; no data to record how many eyes see the keyword 'good' or 'outstanding' and correlate this to the school name and their logos.
>
> Think on a large scale: 25,000 schools hoping to 'go to print' ready for the publicity shot in the local paper and a 20-foot vinyl banner is pinned across the school gates for all to see. There are only two organisations making any return on investment here. One, the printing companies. Two, Ofsted: they get a boost to their long-term viability amid an ever-increasing call for reform, validity and better value for money.

> The Association of School and College Leaders (ASCL) shares its advice to members in the shape of '101 ideas to help you manage inspection'. Number 91 reads:
>
> > Reconsider your banner: whilst you may be proud of your inspection result, remember Ofsted is not the only mark of success. Perhaps the views of your pupils and parents would be a refreshing and welcome alternative!
>
> In the remaining parts of the chapter, Helen will put forward a good case to explain why 'teacher retention rates and the number seeking to train are falling'. The more difficult question is how to change this pattern.

The invisible school culture is the reality behind the veneer and the real-life experience you would get if you worked there. It is the lived experience of the outward-facing mission statement; and, sadly for some settings, it is often only when you work there that you get a true sense of what it is like.

The invisible school culture may be a challenge to see but it is not impossible to catch glimpses. It is the gut feeling you get when you walk in the door; the sense of atmosphere; the way that every person you deal with treats you. You can tell a lot from speaking to the secretary when you sign in: if you are ignored, spoken to abruptly or overhear negative gossip then that is an indication that the invisible school culture is not healthy. I once sat in a school as a visitor. The secretary had no idea where I was from, simply that I was visiting the inclusion manager. Whilst I was sat there waiting for my appointment, a parent and pupil arrived and joined me. The pupil was clearly upset about leaving his mother and was showing signs of distress. He began to cry and this escalated to shouts and screams when staff came to physically remove him to his classroom. As his mother left, the secretary turned to me and said, 'That is the god-awful sound I have to listen to every day from him. That child is a nightmare.' The school's mission statement included the line 'warm and sensitive approach'.

A school culture does not remain static; it is constantly shifting and changing depending on the people and politics at play. Any changes to the culture occur in different ways and for different reasons. Some changes may be evolutionary in nature. These are unconscious and unplanned for and might include a gradual turnover of staff bringing new ideas or the slow change in the socio-economic status of pupils attending the school. However, some changes are transformative and these are conscious and deliberate acts. These may include a change to the values and beliefs held by the school due to a new headteacher or a change in political policy. Jessica's and Martyn's stories in Chapters 7 and 8 remind us how much a school can change with a new leader at the helm.

In the short term, school cultures tend to be self-sustaining unless either of the types of changes discussed above comes into play. This self-sustaining nature is due to the fact that new staff to the school will largely model the behaviours seen in existing staff (Prosser, 1999). If we accept the wisdom that 'good seeds grow in strong cultures' (Saphier and King, 1985) then it is logical that even the best seeds will struggle in hostile cultures. This is the basis of every toxic school: a culture which doesn't allow good seeds to flourish.

Creation – dark personalities

People with dark personalities can be said to have a mixture of a triad of characteristics: narcissism, Machiavellianism and psychopathy. This can make them disagreeable people to try and work alongside (Paulhus and Williams, 2002). These characteristics have a degree of overlap and but we will look at them separately before trying to understand how they can combine to make a dark personality.

Narcissists are those who think that everything is, or should be, about them. They lack empathy for colleagues and pupils, come across as arrogant, and believe they are beyond repute. A narcissistic teacher will try and exercise their power over people without feeling the need to explain their decisions; they will expect you to comply with their request simply because they are the ones who have asked. They are the teachers who try to dominate the NQTs or new staff by asserting their authority in relation to picking the prime playground duty days or dictating who can sit where in the staffroom. They are the teachers who seemingly always have someone running around on their behalf photocopying or always direct others to do parts of their role that they don't enjoy.

Machiavellians are expert manipulators. They are those who plan and plot using their colleagues as pieces in a game of chess they are solely in control of. A Machiavellian teacher keeps their own counsel in all things; they might elicit your views and opinions on the new deputy head or a new policy but you will leave the conversation without any idea what they thought. They will seek your friendship because of what you can offer them rather than out of mutual respect; if you can be a useful ally in their grand scheme then they will want to keep you close. Their schemes are naturally those that suit their own needs: it need not be aiming for leadership but could be as simple as keeping the year group they enjoy teaching or making sure their lessons are in the best places on the timetable.

Psychopaths mask their negative traits with a veneer of normalcy. They are dishonest and act without conscience, often for the pleasure it gives them. A psychopathic teacher is utterly charming to you and to everyone around them and can appear to show the full range of emotional responses. Yet this outward presentation is an act; their real purpose is to gain enjoyment from the situations they are creating, even if that means walking all over you. A psychopathic teacher will be the one who turns your idea into their idea without you noticing until it is too late. They are the teachers who listen to your concerns in confidence and then share them with the people involved. They are the ultimate 'snakes in suits' (Babiak and Hare, 2007).

It goes without saying that we can all probably act in the ways described above on occasion. The difference is that people with a darker personality tend to act like that for the majority of the time, which can lead to the creation of a toxic workplace. Having to deal with work colleagues like this is draining and can be demoralising. Brendan's experiences in chapter 5 highlight how disastrous it can be to get on the wrong side of a teacher with a dark personality.

We should note that some of these traits can have a positive elements that actually *benefit* a workplace. For example, someone who has a narcissistic personality may be a very conscientious worker, which means that they are super organised when planning that Key Stage 3 trip to Disneyland Paris or their Special Educational Needs (SEN) Support Plans are perfect. There are many teachers with darker personalities and that means they are likely to be in every school. Their negative impact is often reduced by careful leadership and an awareness of their tendencies. However, there comes a problem when our school leaders are not able to manage challenging staff like this; they may have a darker personality themselves or they may be ineffective as a leader. So what do we do when leadership actually contributes to our schools' toxicity?

Creation – leadership

Leadership can be said to have two main functions: to provide direction and exercise influence (Leithwood and Riehl, 2003). Successful school leaders do this in a positive and affirming way through the development and establishment of core values which enable learners to succeed and staff to flourish. There are many types of positive school leadership. One of these is distributed leadership, which is a shared leadership between those in formal roles that allows other staff to develop their own capacity as leaders (Sheppard et al., 2010). A second example of positive leadership is known as instructional leadership, whereby the skill and charisma of the leadership is used effectively to engage with staff, encourage teacher development and have a transparent approach to their role (Blase and Blase, 2000). In these examples, the leaders know the culture of their school and the needs of individual staff within it, and are able to create spaces for those they lead to develop and evaluate where the school is heading; the social climate is strong and staff feel valued and respected (Skaalvik and Skaalvik, 2011). These are the types of schools where staff are supported to develop within their roles, obtain further professional qualifications, and have their efforts acknowledged and praised.

However, anecdotally, we know that leaders can also display negative behaviours which can severely impact upon the way that a school functions on a day-to-day basis. We have probably all experienced (or at least heard) stories of teachers working for school leaders who are distant, impersonal, arrogant, or manipulative (as discussed above when we looked at dark personalities in teachers). The real problem with leaders is when they actively use these dark personality traits without anyone to rein them in. These are the types of schools where staff and learners are seen as inanimate pieces in an educational game of chess rather than as real people. Negative leadership like this lacks the moral purpose which is so critical to Fullan's understanding of a positive school leader (Fullan, 2002). This moral purpose has both macro and micro interpretations: on a macro level, it is about making a positive social difference in society; whereas at a micro level, it is simply how leaders treat everyone that they work with. 'Moral purpose' hints at the need for leaders to be ethical; those without ethics and a moral purpose border on being part of the darker side of education with a dark personality as defined above.

In *The Dark Side of Transformational Leadership*, Dennis Tourish investigates how the charisma of some leaders can create a climate in which followers become powerless to speak out or feed back criticism to the leader through fear or duty (Tourish, 2013). This can then lead to a cycle whereby the lack of critical feedback is used by the leader to justify their position, which is then enforced with even more rigour: 'No one has complained so I am just going to carry on as I have been.' For the staff within the school, sharing their professional voice becomes harder because it will be seen to be critical of the accepted status quo and a challenge to authority. Even if staff do speak out, there can be a tendency by some leaders to ignore such criticism and instead become more determined to enact their ideas: they cannot possibly be wrong. In both cases there is a real lack of space and appreciation for professional voice (which will be discussed later in chapter 11).

This type of toxic leadership can be born of a leader joining a setting where such leadership practices are already prevalent or inherent in the leader themselves. In both cases, the personality and identity of the leader is important. In the former, the school seeks to appoint a new leader based on their ability to keep the status quo; they are often brought up through the ranks and trained in the ethos of the school before eventually taking up post. (One school I worked with who took this line of leadership talked of new heads being 'anointed not appointed' due to the careful years of preparation that went into developing and shaping staff who had been earmarked for succession.) In the latter, where the toxicity is within the leader themselves, they accept a position and then, driven by their own personality, use their position of power to exert their influence.

Tourish's discussions of the American energy corporation Enron and the cult leader Jim Jones show examples of these different types of toxic leadership (Tourish, 2013). Within Enron, those appointed to positions of leadership were carefully selected and chosen because of their ability to continue the company vision and to reinforce the carefully constructed cultural norms, ultimately leading to the company's collapse in 2001. In comparison, Jim Jones used his charisma and power to influence those who would eventually join him in the Peoples Temple, transforming it from a left wing church involved in political activism to a cultic movement which ended in the murders/suicides of 918 people in 1978.

These examples are extreme and by no means am I trying to say that leadership in education is in the same vein. However, the experiences of leadership that they highlight are worth mentioning for several reasons. Firstly, we can witness dilute versions of their failings in many schools. We can all think of charismatic headteachers who staff seem to follow blindly or an SLT where everyone appears to be cut from the same cloth. Secondly, we should not look at school leadership in isolation as if it were a totally unique entity; leadership positions in every setting – be it a company or a hospital – share common traits, including those that can lead to the development of toxic cultures and workplaces. What makes educational leadership unique is the direct impact that it can have on some of the most vulnerable members of society: the learners who access the schools such leaders manage.

Effect - learners

The simple truth is that schools are about learners. They are places where hopes and aspirations are developed and they have the ability to make or break a person depending upon the experiences they provide. There is an important point that needs to be clarified here: there are a range of schools where the needs of learners are not the primary focus, and it is important to understand how these fit in with our understanding of toxic schools.

There is a growing swath of schools where learners may be the *public* reason for their existence but the under-culture is one of generating money or self-service to the careers of those who run them. They are schools where education happens like a factory and the manufactured output is a fully formed pupil. These schools are wolves in sheep's clothing and they may be run by local authorities or academies, or be free schools. They may be state funded or private, mainstream or special.

Regardless of what type they are, there is a sense within them that the learners are secondary to the school itself rather than being seen as the reason for the school's existence. Whilst I disagree with the idea that a focus on money or personal achievement has any place in teaching, these schools cannot automatically be labelled as being toxic. Many such schools do provide a school culture and climate where learners and staff thrive and this needs to be acknowledged. So whilst some of these schools *may* be deemed toxic, it is not true that all of them are.

Toxic schools are settings where the created climate and treatment of staff directly affect the wellbeing and outcomes of the children and young people who attend them. The reason I became a teacher was out of a motivation to work with and for children. Although some have criticised the teaching profession for being institutionalised and made up of people who have little drive to move from being a learner to leading the learning (Fuller and Bown, 1975), I personally felt that my desire to teach was inspired by my own experiences of being a learner.

Take a moment to think about your favourite experience as a learner at school. Think about the staff who worked there, the activities you did and the experiences you had. Like many, I had both disastrous times and others that were pure enjoyment. When I look back at my own past, and the teachers that I can recall, I have mixed feelings. Yet it was these experiences which led me to develop a belief system for how I should be as a teacher (Pajares, 1992; Mitchell and Weber, 2003). This belief system is based on having a genuine relationship between teacher and pupil learners within a safe, inclusive and supportive school. My own educational journey had one amazing teacher – Mr Thomas – and one awful experience – Mrs Cook. The following is an autoethnographical account of my relationship with each of them.

> In the summer term of Year 4, one dramatic event happened that affected me greatly: I changed schools. It was not a natural move because it happened neither at the end of an academic year nor due to a house move. Instead, it was a mid-term move due to my parents' dissatisfaction with the school I had been at since I was an infant – a school that slowly chipped away at my spirit until I was a shadow of the child I had previously been.
>
> The school was not a primary school but an infant and junior school. Both buildings were large; the school had been built in the 1960s with large windows and shiny wooden floors. The demography was predominantly white and the catchment area encompassed a rambling estate of the same age as the school, with a mixture of private and council housing. I spent several years at the school and had never had a memorable time; the school had a cold and unfriendly feel. The headteacher was distant and did not seem to be involved in any of the day-to-day events. Mrs Cook was the name of my teacher in Year 4. She was an older lady, a handful of years away from retirement, stout and matronly with grey short hair swept back into dramatic curls. She wore pleated dresses – often in bold colours like royal blue or British racing green – with a small black belt. She was an indomitable force and very early on in the year I had felt her wrath over my spelling. I had always struggled with spelling and tables, but I had never felt that my lack of ability was a cause for concern. Yet in that autumn term I was faced with

two words that became my nemesis: 'rabbit' and 'tractor'. Mrs Cook progressed from leaving angry red-pen messages marching like an invading army across my page to shouting verbal messages across the classroom like a sergeant major.

Mrs Cook terrorised the whole class but I felt that a special form of malice was reserved for me. When James stole my shoes and hid them after PE, I was branded a liar for denying any part in their disappearance. I walked up and down the parquet floor in my knee-high socks, crying, unable to make sense of the rabbit hole I had found myself in. Hidden in a white PE crate at the back of the storage area, I found my shoes. By this time it was the end of the school day so I slipped my shoes on and traipsed miserably down the path connecting the two schools to where my lift was waiting. I can recall feeling dejected; I had never experienced being disliked before and I could not rationalise why I was so. Of course I had fallen out with friends and had had disagreements with family, but they were short lived and did not last long in the memory. This was different; I was a powerless child and Mrs Cook held all the cards. Not used to being disliked, I tried the only tactic I knew, which was to try to be liked; to befriend her and make her see who I really was rather than the misconceptions she clearly held of me. Due to a childhood illness, I was small for my age; and I had been brought up to act confident and trust in my own abilities. By nature I was a diplomat and tried to forge a middle path that would lead to peace, if not reconciliation.

I had received a leather bound copy of *The Railway Children* by Edith Nesbit for Christmas and had taken it into school to be our class reader as a means of gaining favour with her. I wanted her to be thankful, to notice that I was entrusting her with this very special gift because I respected her. It did not work. The class sat enthralled with her dramatic reading style, yet I gained no truce. I will never know why she disliked me so much. Maybe I was an easy victim; maybe I reminded her of someone else. Even as an adult, these feelings of helplessness and worthlessness lingered; Mrs Cook had created room for doubt to creep into my childish world. My parents refused to let me stay any longer. Even on my last day, Mrs Cook continued to exert her power as she refused to let me say goodbye to my friends, instead requesting that I empty my tray in silence and wait in reception to be collected. Watching my mother arrive through the double glass doors was pure salvation. The head was indifferent to her questions, simply saying, 'What do you expect me to do?' I left the school with nothing other than memories and hurt.

After half term, I arrived at my new school. It had a link with the local RAF base so there was a high turnover of children from the furthest side of the globe. Some children stayed for a term; others for a few years. The school was led by a headteacher who was dedicated and passionate. He would dress in a gorilla costume and walk the corridors simply because it made the children laugh. He would cancel lessons when it snowed so that our many international students would get a chance to experience running around in the cold whiteness of the season. He was visible and involved and staff smiled and laughed with him. This attitude influenced the whole staff team. Some raised money for a computer room by completing the Three Peaks Challenge. Some would put on lavish productions twice a year and some ran numerous clubs and activities in their own time. The ethos of the school was one of inclusion, enjoyment and learning. If it sounds idyllic then that is because it was.

The classroom which I found myself in was radically at odds from the one I had left. I had arrived midway through a term and therefore midway through a topic. My new class were embarking on a project to recreate the Bayeux Tapestry on the walls of the classroom. I was greeted by Mr Thomas, a young moustached teacher who always smelt faintly of coffee. He turned out to be my biggest inspiration, and the time I spent in his class, in Year 4 and then Year 5, was a wonderful experience. At my previous school, my handwriting had been printed and only in pencil; but now I had fallen into a world of fountain pens and cursive writing. Mr Thomas quickly realised the problem and spent time working with me to perfect my joins.

> Presentation of my handwriting was never my strong point but he was able to see beyond that to the content of what I was saying. He fostered a true love of learning; and when I think about my school years, many of the experiences that come to mind are those spent with him.

What have I learnt from these experiences as an adult and a teacher? Mrs Cook taught me the power that teachers and schools can have and how easily it can be abused (Ingersoll, 1996; Shumba, 2007). From her I realised that it is possible to damage a child quickly and leave lasting scars and memories. What Mr Thomas taught me is more obvious but no less important. He showed me the power that building a relationship can bring, that learning is not solely about what happens in the classroom – it is wider, broader and more exciting. Most of all, I learnt that the ethos and values of a school can leave a lasting imprint on the learners that attend: one situation shaped me to be subservient and powerless, whilst the other encouraged me to be more individualistic and free.

As previously discussed, staff who are motivated by access to continued professional development create a better climate for learning (Day, 2002). These staff are engaged with their work, seeing it as fulfilling and worthwhile. They are motivated and, due to the fact that they feel skilled to deal with all aspects of their role, are less likely to take time off with work-related stress due to feeling unable to cope with the wide variety of needs presented by some learners. Put simply: a happy and healthy workforce means happier and healthier learners. Research published in January 2018 by Leeds Beckett University found that 77% of teachers felt that their own mental health was having a detrimental impact on pupil progress. So what about the effect of toxic schools on teachers?

Effect – teachers

Barely a day goes by without a news article or a story shared on social media about teachers and mental health. The Office for National Statistics (ONS) published data in March 2017 for the years 2011 to 2015 for suicide rates based upon occupation. Of the 102 recorded suicides of those in education, 73% were of primary or nursery school teachers. Whilst I do not claim that each of these tragic stories is directly related to teaching, the fact that the ONS identified this fact as one of its key findings is surely testament to how staggering it is. Although suicide is an extremely uncommon reaction to stress, research published by Leeds Beckett University discussed above also highlighted that of the 775 teachers surveyed, 52% had been diagnosed by a GP as having a mental health need.

It is no wonder that teacher retention rates and the number seeking to train are falling. The House of Commons Briefing Paper 7222 from January 19th 2018 shows that Initial Teacher Training (ITT) recruitment for the year 2017–18 was below target for secondary education across all subjects except history and PE (Physical Education). The paper also states that 50,110 left the profession between November 2015 and November 2016, leaving a gap of 2620 more teachers leaving than joining. It must be remembered that not every trainee teacher stays on in the profession and there is a natural number of teachers leaving each year due to retirement. That said, the system is in crisis.

Teachers are more than people who work in classrooms. The impact of mental health needs on staff affects their relationships and family lives, and it is these stories that are central to this book. Some of those you will hear from have suffered mental health concerns directly related to their teaching roles: in chapter 4, we hear Richard's experience of how teaching led to mental health concerns; in chapter 6, Gwen found that the stress of her PGCE (Postgraduate Certificate in Education) meant that she had to rely upon support from her husband due to the breakdown she had suffered on a placement; and in chapter 8, Martyn experienced mental health issues which could have progressed if he had not resigned from post.

What is it about teaching that causes so much damage to so many staff? There can be an assumption from those outside the profession that teaching is easy: leave work at 3pm and have 13 weeks' paid holiday. For those working within the system, this is laughable. Teaching is a profession where you are under constant scrutiny both as an individual and as a collective. The goalposts constantly move and the expectation of what duties you must perform outside of the hours you are paid for is huge. There is often a frustration among teachers that we are in a profession which is largely misunderstood by those on the outside. Where the latter see 3pm finishes and holidays, teachers see hours of unpaid work, often using their own resources and eating into their lives outside of the classroom. The problem has become one where there is simply not enough time in the paid week for teachers to complete the tasks they need to do in order to fulfil their role.

This is not to say that there are not stresses and strains in any other job; we all know of people who have experienced mental health needs and are not teachers. The difference is that teaching requires you to work at 100% of your ability, every hour of every day of every week that there are young people in your class. There is no room for slippage: failure to keep up with the pace can be like setting off the first domino in a very long chain. It is also a job where there is always something else you could do before you finish for the day; you never seem to really compete anything. Teaching often feels like survival of the fittest.

Toxic schools are those which turn an already challenging job into one which can feel like a Herculean task.

Bibliography

Babiak, P. and Hare, R. D. (2007) *Snakes in suits.* New York, NY: HarperCollins.

Baumeister, R. F. and Leary, M. R. (1995) 'The need to belong: desire for interpersonal attachments as a fundamental human motivation, *Psychological Bulletin* 117 (3) pp. 497–529.

Blase, J. and Blase, J. (2000) 'Effective instructional leadership: teachers' perspectives on how principals promote teaching and learning in schools', *Journal of Educational Administration* 38 (2) pp. 130–141.

Chun, R. & Davies, G. (2001) 'E-reputation: the role of mission and vision statements in positioning strategy', *Journal of Brand Management* 8 (4) pp. 315–333.

Day, C. (2002) 'School reform and transitions in teacher professionalism and identity', *International Journal of Educational Research* 37 (8) pp. 677–692.

Fritz, R. (1996) *Corporate tides: the inescapable laws of organizational structure.* Oakland, CA: Berrett-Koehler Publishers.

Fullan, M. (2002) 'Principals as leaders in a culture of change', *Educational Leadership* 59 (8) pp. 16–21.

Fuller, F. F. and Bown, O. H. (1975) 'Becoming a teacher' in Ryan, K. (ed.) *Teacher education: the seventy-fourth yearbook of the National Society for the Study of Education, part 2.* Chicago, IL: University of Chicago Press, pp. 25–52.

Ingersoll, R. M. (1996) 'Teachers' decision-making power and school conflict', *Sociology of Education* 69 (2) pp. 159–176.

Leithwood, K. A. and Riehl, C. (2003) *What we know about successful school leadership.* Philadelphia, PA: Laboratory for Student Success, Temple University.

Mitchell, C. and Weber, S. (2003) *Reinventing ourselves as teachers: beyond nostalgia.* Abingdon: Routledge.

Pajares, M. F. (1992) 'Teachers' beliefs and educational research: cleaning up a messy construct', *Review of Educational Research* 62 (3) pp. 307–332.

Paulhus, D. L. and Williams, K. M. (2002) 'The dark triad of personality: narcissism, Machiavellianism, and psychopathy', *Journal of Research in Personality* 36 (6) pp. 556–563.

Prosser, J. (1999) *School culture.* Thousand Oaks, CA: SAGE Publications.

Rosenberg, M. (1977) 'Contextual dissonance effects: nature and causes', *Psychiatry* 40 (3) pp. 205–217.

Rozycki, E. G. (2004) 'Mission and vision in education', *Educational Horizons* 82 (2) pp. 94–98.

Saphier, J. and King, M. (1985) 'Good seeds grow in strong cultures', *Educational Leadership* 42 (6) pp. 67–74.

Sheppard, B., Hurley, N. and Dibbon, D. (2010) 'Distributed leadership, teacher morale, and teacher enthusiasm: unravelling the leadership pathways to school success', *American Educational Research Association annual conference.* Denver, CO, 30th April – 4th May.

Shumba, A. (2007) 'Emotional abuse in the classroom: a cultural dilemma?', *Journal of Emotional Abuse* 4 (3–4) pp. 139–149.

Skaalvik, E. M. & Skaalvik, S. (2011) 'Teacher job satisfaction and motivation to leave the teaching profession: relations with school context, feeling of belonging, and emotional exhaustion', *Teaching and Teacher Education* 27 (6) pp. 1029–1038.

Stoll, L. and Fink, D. (1996) *Changing our schools: linking school effectiveness and school improvement.* Maidenhead: Open University Press.

Tourish, D. (2013) *The dark side of transformational leadership: a critical perspective.* Abingdon: Routledge.

Reflections

Chapter 3 - Ethnography and autoethnography: the use of narratives and fictionalised narratives

In this fascinating chapter we start to understand how Helen has conducted her research, as well as the differences between ethnographical and autoethnographical approaches, which ought to be of great interest to educators who are immersed in action learning. We also discover how and why 'personal narratives' have validity in education and should be treated as a reliable source of research – something education ministers will find difficult.

As Professor Becky Allen and Dr. Sam Sims write in *The Teacher Gap* (2018), 'time in the classroom is a powerful enhancer'; yet 'teaching can be aptly described as an ill-structured problem precisely because most decisions faced by teachers are too idiosyncratic to be categorised'.

Here lies our problem within the education sector. The complex work that a teacher does in their own classroom, their professional judgement or wisdom, cannot be successfully measured. Politicians tried desperately to find an easy methodology to report back to taxpayers; and if you are a school leader working at the thinner end of the wedge where your own career is at risk, then you will do absolutely everything within your power to ensure that you can measure the complex work that teachers do in your own school – even if this results in a toxic culture becoming the norm.

Before we hear the narratives of the teachers involved, it is important to explain how these stories were created and to understand how ethnography, autoethnography, and fictionalisation were used to allow them to tell the truth of their experiences whilst remaining anonymous.

What is ethnography?

Ethnography is a form of research based around engaging with people. Derived from two Greek words – *ethnos*, meaning 'people', and *grapho*, meaning 'I write' – it is a broad term for a range of different ways which we can write about the social lives and experiences of real people. The end result leaves us with rich accounts that often include the perspectives of the person who has been the observer (O'Reilly, 2008).

Historically, ethnography has a somewhat murky past. Often associated with colonisation and empire-building, the first type of ethnographical writing was conducted by Herodotus, who wrote his book *Histories* describing the culture and political values of the countries around him. The colonisation of other countries by Spain, Portugal, France, and England from the late Middle Ages continued the trend of recording the lives of indigenous peoples, often in a patronising or derogatory way (Clair, 2003).

However, don't let that put you off – it is the later development of the form in both Britain and Chicago which had a greater impact on the modern use. Although early 20th-century British ethnographers were still associated with colonialism, the thought process behind much of their work was to immerse themselves in the cultures they were observing and try to understand them. This was then further developed in America by the Chicago School, where there was a desire to try to understand the groups who were on the margins of the industrial boom in the 1920s and '30s. Both the British and the American forms had developed ethnography into a study by someone who became an *active insider* in the groups they were observing rather than an outsider who could be deemed to be passing judgement.

Modern ethnography is therefore a method which researchers use to understand the deep reality of a social situation as only those who directly experience it can understand. This is something which other forms of research simply cannot achieve to the same degree. Imagine trying to use some of the different methods available to describe the school you work in. You could use quantitative numerical data on the types of learners in your setting to describe how many have special needs, are on free school meals, or break down the learners into different ethnic backgrounds. You could ask staff to complete questionnaires on their educational background, whether they have a traditional or progressive view of education, or how they rate the school on a 1–10 scale. Whilst this gives a snapshot of learners and staff, to me it raises so many questions: what impact does the number of Traveller children have on the culture of the school? How does the teacher who describes themselves as very progressive cope in a setting where the other staff generally term themselves to be traditionalist? How are the high numbers of SEN learners supported and do the staff feel that they have adequate training to do the best job they can? What is the backstory of the grammar school teacher who came from a very working-class background and attended a low-achieving comprehensive school?

This is where I believe that an ethnographical approach has a lot to offer as it encourages us to ask those questions and to dig deeper to find the rich stories which are contained under the surface. When we apply these principles to our own lives, and share our personal experiences, we are writing autoethnography.

What is autoethnography?

Autoethnography can be described as a personal challenge that allows an individual voice to have an impact at a wider sociological level (Wall,

2008). There are examples of autoethnography found across a variety of disciplines including nursing and social work (Kanuha, 2000). It is simple to state what the term literally means: it is writing (-graphy) in a personal way (auto-) to understand a culture/society (-ethno-). However, there are a range of interpretations of the term with no single agreed understanding.

This also is true of how autoethnography is used within education, leaving many variations in style and format. For some, the self-reflection in autoethnography is akin to the self-reflection that teachers need to fulfil their role (Hayler, 2010). For others, it is the direct impact that it could have on professional practice and its ability to impact upon social change that give it credibility as a tool (Starr, 2010). From a personal point of view, I have found it most useful to reflect upon 'the space between' my teaching and my pupils (Dwyer and Buckle, 2009), which I also understood to be similar to that found within my relationships with staff. This elusive space – accessible by reflection leading to personal and professional consequences – was what I inadvertently discovered through my research and this was what subsequently dominated my thesis. I had found emancipation in the experimental autoethnography highlighted by the chance discovery of a book by Carolyn Ellis called *The Ethnographic I* whilst searching on Amazon (Ellis, 2004). In this book, Ellis describes teaching a course on autoethnography to a fictionalised group of students. A large portion of her career had been devoted to developing the field of autoethnography and this included writing intimately about her own life, including family deaths and an abortion (Ellis, 2009). Her earlier book was one that I simply devoured as it resonated so much with what I felt inside.

There are naturally other opinions on autoethnography; it is not universally accepted as a credible method for academic writing and is regularly criticised. During my research for my thesis, I discovered an openly controversial (although brief) response outlining six major criticisms which are important to respect and address:

1. Autoethnography cannot fight familiarity.
2. Autoethnography is hard to publish ethically.

3. Autoethnography lacks analysis.
4. Autoethnography is focused on those in power, not the powerless.
5. Autoethnography removes the need for us to go out and get data.
6. 'We' are simply not interesting enough to write about.

(Delamont, 2007)

Delamont elaborated on this further with a comparison about her research into the Afro-Brazilian martial art capoeira and personal moments of crisis; she maintained that her personal crises did not add any new knowledge to her research (Delamont, 2009). Yet I believe that these small moments of crisis are valid as they can make up the 'space between' discussed above (Starr, 2010). Our experiences of events can add to the wider knowledge on a subject and the very act of becoming self-aware can have an impact on wider societal issues (Yang, 2012). Our self-awareness can impact on how we manage not only relationships with pupils but also relationships with staff.

Delamont's concerns about ethics are important; however, these were based upon the assumption that all other forms of research are *easy* to publish ethically. Personally I agree with Ellis's defence of autoethnographical ethics and her belief that we needed to be accountable for what we write and accept that it may challenge those who read it as well as challenging ourselves when we write it; one should approach autoethnographic research with honesty and integrity (Ellis, 2004). Delamont raised a further concern regarding the ethics of writing about individuals and the ease with which they could be identified in autoethnographic writing (Delamont, 2007). This is an issue that Ellis faced in the years after her research into the fisherfolk of Maryland and Virginia (Ellis, 2009). This was one argument of Delamont's that I agree with, which is why I make use of fictionalisation in both my own writing and in my presentation of the autoethnographical writing of the teachers in this book.

Regarding her criticisms on analysis, I agree in part that some of the more emotional autoethnographic writing available to read – such as that by Ellis working with a cancer patient (Ellis, 1998) – is not readily open to deep analysis. However, this was not the case for all autoethnographical research: Anderson has comprehensively argued that autoethnography can be analytical. His five key principles were an attempt to encourage those interested in autoethnography to move away from purely evocative writing (Anderson, 2006).

As a counter to the criticisms of Delamont, I offer four defences of authoethnography. Firstly, there is the sheer accessibility of a well-written piece of autoethnographic writing into worlds that have been previously hidden (Boyle and Parry, 2007). When relating this to schools, we are able to enter into hidden places behind classroom doors and meet people whom we previously had no knowledge of. Secondly, writing in an autoethnographic style allows us to link the personal with wider cultural and societal issues (Holt, 2008). This means that we can situate the individual experiences of teachers within the wider worlds in which they exist. Thirdly, choosing to write about your own experiences can offer a different approach from the long-held dominance of more scientific forms of research (Wall, 2008); the stories told by teachers can be used to support data as well as being an inspiration to generate data on issues which may appear, such as teacher recruitment and retention. Finally, in writing about ourselves, we enter into a relationship of trust with whoever reads what we write: we need their belief in us to validate our experiences. This is termed 'authorial honesty' by Pat Sikes (Sikes, 2012). For teachers writing in this way, it is about aiding the development of a profession based upon trust and collaboration with a view to understanding and supporting each other better.

What are narratives?

Stories are how we learn the history of our families, of our culture, of world events; they are how we pass on moral teachings, and how we are instructed into society; they allow us to link different events and experiences so that we can make sense of the world around us (Kramp,

2003). Narratives are collections of these stories linked together to share a perspective on life events. Narrative is a form of expression and communication (Coste, 1990); it is fundamentally part of our humanity. We tell stories every day; just think about how often throughout the day you retell a story to a colleague, learner or family member; think of how often a song lyric or event reminds you of a story you have in your memories. As humans, we think about and tell our stories every day, from those short relations of a single event to those long retellings of a disastrous date. We tell stories verbally, through writing, and through action. The whole of human life is an extended narrative communicated in a multitude of ways to a seemingly never-ending audience. Our stories can often work as an internal framework to support our understanding of new experiences.

Narratives are often criticised for placing too much emphasis on the individual instead of the wider social context that individuals exist within (Connelly and Clandinin, 1990). Whilst in some cases this may be valid, it could be argued that looking at the individual experience of a cultural or social process can actually shed light on the process itself and how it affects individual life experiences (Nelson, 2003). The stories that the teachers tell in the following chapters do not represent the experiences of *everyone* working in a school, nor do they act as a full critique of the wider education system. Instead they are the lived experiences of some teachers that can help us to raise questions about the wider culture of education within our current system.

What are fictionalised narratives?

The term 'fictionalised narratives' was not something I encountered as a teacher until I had started to research for my doctoral thesis. I quickly realised what a useful tool it was in allowing teachers, and pupils, to share their stories in an anonymous and highly ethical way. Sometimes called ethnographic fiction (Davis and Ellis, 2008) or fictionalised ethnography (Reed, 2011), these narratives enable stories from the silenced and excluded to be heard (Sparkes, 1997). This is true of teachers working in toxic schools. It should be noted that the use of any speech marks in the following teacher stories is not to report exact speech but is part of a fictionalised narratives approach, as is the sharing of sensitive information, through stories which are generated in part by the author and not solely by the teller (Clough, 2002).

A lot of the information from the teachers who took part was sensitive and potentially damaging to their careers or personal lives. There was a natural hesitancy to share such personal stories, especially as many of them had never been shared with anyone before. By creating anonymised stories and backgrounds for each teacher, their privacy was protected. However there was more to this than simply changing the names of people and places. Fictionalised narratives can be compared to historical novels: both are about events that it is agreed *did* happen, yet these events are presented in a way imagined by the author (Hecht, 2007). This makes them useful when dealing with highly sensitive or ethically questionable data, as Andrew Sparkes discusses when sharing narratives about homosexuality (Sparkes, 1997). These fictionalised narratives allow a picture to be painted of each experience, making the teachers real, so that anyone reading their narratives can have a clear image in their minds of the storyteller and develop a sense of empathy with the characters and their experiences (Wallace, 2010). Yet they also allow for stories of other teachers to be linked in. These are teachers who did not feel able to share the details of their full career but wanted, in some way, to give of themselves to benefit others. Therefore the five narratives presented are a composite of a variety of different professional lives and experiences woven together.

Issues of interpretation and 'truth'

There are, of course, a multitude of different 'truths' for any given story: a story could be historically true, or psychologically true; it could be a faithful relation of a memory or the retelling of someone else's perspective. It is important to remember that narratives do not claim to offer a universal *truth*; instead, their truth lies in the telling of a story which is internally acceptable to the teller in that place or time (Sandelowski, 1991). The narratives in the following chapters are therefore 'true' for those telling them.

It is important to remember that narratives are not always reliable: tellers exaggerate, manipulate or are 'creative' in their expression of events (Fitzpatrick, 2015). We admonish small children for 'telling tales' as if the generation of a story is negative. Yet we then tell our own tales, which change and adapt, often without us being aware; we create a narrative we are at peace with (McAdams and McLean, 2013). All of the teachers involved in telling their stories are doing so from a point of reflection and in a way that they are comfortable with. If they had told their stories soon after the events discussed, or to a close friend, then I am sure there would have been other points recalled and slightly different perspectives given. There will therefore be events which have not been recorded either because they have been forgotten or because they are too painful to remember.

The stories the teachers in this book tell are not claiming to be *historically* true (Hecht, 2007). You couldn't do an internet search and find any of the schools they worked in; nor could you scour the local papers for anecdotes they mention. Instead, their stories share a moment in time, a snapshot of how the teachers perceived the world at a specific point of reflection. They are written in a fictionalised way and are blended with the stories of others to develop certain points and give greater depth.

Fictionalised narratives and education

Narratives can help us to tell the 'truth' of a situation or relationship whilst respecting the privacy of those involved (Reed, 2011). Narratives are important as they can give people a voice where previously they may have been silenced (Merrill and West, 2009). Goodson, when discussing the stories of teachers, explained that their voices are often unheard and teachers are silenced, as those with less power are only able to tell a portion of a story; wider perspectives are only available to those with greater power (Goodson, 1994). On a practical level, it means that teachers' stories of their professional lives often go untold because there is a great risk that they will be countered, downplayed or explained away by those with greater power and authority; teachers are often a lone voice whispering into a storm.

The teachers involved in telling their narratives in the following chapters have largely kept the events private out of a fear that they may face repercussions in their careers from those with more power. Many had not told close family or friends the full details but this was largely due to shame, guilt, or a desire to preserve some strength and dignity in their personal lives.

Fictionalisation has been used in professional education stories to anonymise real people, schools and local authorities whilst they are based on real people and events (Fellows, 2001). This use of fictionalisation has enabled teaching professionals to write about challenging and emotional situations and to share stories that people have wanted to tell to a wider audience than they have been able to before, yet remain protected and safe (Clough, 2002). As discussed above, the teachers' stories aim to present the *truth* of what they said but they are also *untrue*, aiming to be between the 'what is' and 'what if' that Reed discusses (Reed, 2011). This space between is how Reed envisages the relationship between writer and storyteller. This relationship is to do with how an *experience* is communicated rather than being a factual chronological account. These narratives are a communication of, and reflection about, the teachers' experiences. They present the truth of what they were willing to divulge in an often factually untrue way.

How the process worked

Initially my interest in toxic schools was inspired by the tweets I had read so it seemed natural to use social media to find teachers who would be willing to share their stories. A variety of social media platforms were used to invite interested teachers to learn more about the project. Following these initial conversations, some teachers naturally decided to withdraw. However, there were many keen to share, which left me with too many participants to include in one book. As it was crucial that the stories were from a cross-section of school settings, each teacher was sent an information sheet about the methods being used. From those who responded, five were selected who not only covered the range of settings but who were prepared to share their stories. Each teacher was given the option of either sharing their story through a semi-structured ethnographic interview or from writing their own autoethnographical account of their experiences as discussed above.

The interviews were very informal, with each teacher choosing a setting where they felt comfortable, such as their own home or a quiet hotel bar. Due to issues of geography, one teacher shared their story through several emails. All the face-to-face interviews were recorded. This was not so that they could be transcribed word for word, as this would have made the stories factual and therefore not fictionalised; it was done to aid in remembering the small details which might otherwise have been missed. The aim was for the storytelling to be natural and not encumbered with too many questions, prompts or technology; it was more like sitting down with a friend rather than a classic interview that many are familiar with from applying for teaching posts. In two cases, over six hours of interviews took place as it took a while to develop a relationship where the teachers felt safe and comfortable enough to tell such personal information. Those who preferred to write their own accounts in the form of an autoethnography (or who wanted to add more information after an interview) were given a basic outline of what they needed to cover but then wrote their account without any other involvement from me. These ethnographic and autoethnographic pieces of writing were then fictionalised.

As part of this fictionalisation process, the teachers were allowed (if they wished) to choose their own name, sex, and geographical location. Some allowed me to do this for them and my choices were then shared. In all cases their school type, career stage and current profession remain as close to the factual truth as possible. After each interview or completion of a piece of autoethnographical writing, the teachers were emailed their fictionalised stories and allowed to comment and request changes until they were confident that the narratives held the truth of their experiences without being factually true to their career history. Some teachers wanted to make many changes whilst others were happy to have shared their experience and left it at that.

Structure of the fictionalised narratives

The following five narratives each follow the same pattern:

- a brief career summary and explanation of the type of settings the teacher was working in
- a detailed background section identifying why and how the teacher joined the profession
- a chronological look at key schools they identified in their career, both toxic and non-toxic
- a detailed look at what made some of their schools toxic with reference to the eight features identified in chapter 1
- a reflective summary

Bibliography

Anderson, L. (2006) 'Analytic autoethnography', *Journal of Contemporary Ethnography* 35 (4) pp. 373–395.

Boyle, M. and Parry, K. (2007) 'Telling the whole story: the case for organizational autoethnography', *Culture and Organization* 13 (3) pp. 185–190.

Clair, R. P. (2003) 'The changing story of ethnography' in Clair, R. P. (ed.) *Expressions of ethnography: novel approaches to qualitative methods.* Albany, NY: State University of New York Press, pp. 3–28.

Clough, P. (2002) *Narratives and fictions in educational research.* Buckingham: Open University Press.

Connelly, F. M. and Clandinin, D. J. (1990) 'Stories of experience and narrative inquiry', *Educational Researcher* 19 (5) pp. 2–14.

Coste, D. (1990) *Narrative as communication.* Minneapolis, MN: University of Minnesota Press.

Davis, C. S. and Ellis, C. (2008) 'Autoethnographic fiction: a method of inquiry' in Liamputtong, P. and Rumbold, J. (eds) *Knowing differently: arts-based and collaborative research methods.* Hauppage, NY: Nova Science Publishers, pp. 99–117.

Delamont, S. (2007) 'Arguments against auto-ethnography', *The British Educational Research Association annual conference.* London, 8th September.

Delamont, S. (2009) 'The only honest thing: autoethnography, reflexivity and small crises in fieldwork', *Ethnography and Education* 4 (1) pp. 51–63.

Dwyer, S. C. and Buckle, J. L. (2009) 'The space between: on being an insider-outsider in qualitative research', *International Journal of Qualitative Methods* 8 (1) pp. 54–63.

Ellis, C. S. (1998) 'Exploring loss through autoethnographic inquiry: autoethnographic stories, co-constructed narratives, and interactive interviews' in Harvey, J. H. (ed.) *Perspectives on loss: a sourcebook.* Abingdon: Routledge, pp. 49–62.

Ellis, C. S. (2004) *The ethnographic I: a methodological novel about autoethnography.* Lanham, MD: Altamira Press.

Ellis, C. S. (2009) *Revision: autoethnographic reflections on life and work.* Abingdon: Routledge.

Fitzpatrick, K. (2015) 'Fiction with friction: unreliable narratives of African American history?', *Diffusion* 8 (1).

Follows, M. (2001) 'Learning from the tale of an Ofsted inspection', *Management in Education* 15 (3) pp. 32–34.

Goodson, I. (1994) 'Studying the teacher's life and work', *Teaching and Teacher Education* 10 (1) pp. 29–37.

Hecht, T. (2007) 'A case for ethnographic fiction', *Anthropology News* 48 (2) pp. 17–18.

Hayler, D. M. (2010) 'Autoethnography: making memory methodology', *Research in Education* 3 (2) pp. 5–9.

Holt, N. L. (2003) 'Representation, legitimation, and autoethnography: an autoethnographic writing story', *International Journal of Qualitative Methods* 2 (1) pp. 18–28.

Kanuha, V. K. (2000) '"Being" native versus "going native": conducting social work research as an insider', *Social Work* 45 (5) pp. 439–447.

McAdams, D. P. and Mclean, K. C. (2013) 'Narrative identity', *Current Directions in Psychological Science* 22 (3) pp. 233–238.

Merrill, B. and West, L. (2009) *Using biographical methods in social research*. Thousand Oaks, CA: SAGE Publications.

Nelson, K. (2003) 'Self and social functions: individual autobiographical memory and collective narrative', *Memory* 11 (2) pp. 125–136.

O'Reilly, K. (2008) *Key concepts in ethnography*. Thousand Oaks, CA: SAGE Publications.

Reed, M. (2011) 'Somewhere between what is and what if: fictionalisation and ethnographic inquiry', *Changing English* 18 (1) pp. 31–43.

Sandelowski, M. (1991) 'Telling stories: narrative approaches in qualitative research', *Journal of Nursing Scholarship* 23 (3) pp. 161–166.

Sikes, P. (2012) 'Truths, truths and treating people properly' in Goodson, I. F., Loveless, A. M. and Stephens, D. (eds) *Explorations in narrative research*. Rotterdam: Sense Publishers, pp. 123–139.

Sparkes, A. C. (1997) 'Ethnographic fiction and representing the absent other', *Sport, Education and Society* 2 (1) pp. 25–40.

Starr, L. J. (2010) 'The use of autoethnography in educational research: locating who we are in what we do', *Canadian Journal for New Scholars in Education* 3 (1) pp. 1–9.

Wall, S. (2008) 'An autoethnography on learning about autoethnography', *International Journal of Qualitative Methods* 5 (2) pp. 146–160.

Wallace, S. (2010) 'Joining the goblins: fictional narratives and the development of student-teachers' reflection on practice in the further education sector', *Educational Action Research* 18 (4) pp. 467–479.

Yang, S. (2012) 'An autoethnography of a childless woman in Korea', *Affilia* 27 (4) pp. 371–380.

Reflections

Chapter 4 - Richard's story

In this chapter we read a story about Richard, who remained in the classroom for less than five years. He is still working within education - but not in the classroom, where we need people like him.

This statistic is well known within the sector and is the one that always reaches the media, but if you dig into the data you will actually start to understand that attrition is at its highest in the first three years of a teacher's career. So although 40 percent of teachers who are working in the classroom leave within the first five years, the most critical moment (where teachers may leave sooner than expected) is in these first two to three years. At what cost to an individual's mental health? At what cost to the taxpayer at large? What hope does a new teacher have if everything that they learn during the training has to stand the test of time over a 10- to 20-year career? If we want to have a world-class education system, we should start by investing much more of our finances, professional development and focus on those teachers in their formative years. We may just keep them for longer. But we may be in a better position to protect teachers from toxic cultures, processes and relationships if more structured coaching and mentoring programmes are in place. If this could be achieved, we would have a better education system for everyone.

Richard's story takes place within primary schools in the North West of England. Richard qualified as a teacher in 2007 and remained within teaching for less than five years, finally leaving to work as a tutor within the prison education service. I first met Richard a few years ago through a mutual acquaintance. I was aware that he had been a teacher but had assumed he had been a mature student leaving the profession because he realised it was not for him. On all the occasions I met him, we never discussed his teaching career and, although he was aware that I was also a teacher, he never asked me about mine. I had found that peculiar as my experience of meeting other teachers in social settings was that we inevitably talked about our jobs.

I had found Richard to be a private and quiet man; he came across as thoughtful and measured. Then, as our personal circumstances changed, we lost contact. We reconnected through Twitter and made passing comments on each other's tweets until I asked for volunteers for this book. He made contact via Twitter, and after a few chats we decided to meet. I asked him to choose a setting where he felt comfortable but he expressed an interest in visiting my house so we arranged a date. Meeting him again after several years was an interesting experience as we were discussing what turned out to be the elephant in the room: his teaching career.

Over an entire afternoon, Richard told his story. At times he was angry, but this was often levelled at himself for he believed that it was his inability to cope, to make appropriate decisions, that had ended his career. However, the most dominant emotion was sadness. On several occasions as he talked, his voice became choked and he struggled to maintain his composure. It was apparent that his attempts to bury his past had not affected the rawness of the emotion.

Richard's story was painful to hear as it told of a passionate teacher existing in a form of educational purgatory, watching friends achieve in a career he would eternally be a spectator of.

Background

I had never intended to be a teacher. I hated school and messed up my A levels, which meant I ended up going to college to try to retake them. The only passion I had in life was IT (Information Technology) so I thought an HND (Higher National Diploma) was the only option I had. The thing was, it was totally different studying IT instead of simply enjoying building and maintaining my own computers or fiddling around networking mates' houses. I just couldn't see myself working in industry; it all seemed so lifeless and dull. My mother, a teacher, suggested I look at teaching as she believed I could really make a go of it. So, that was it; I ended up on a secondary BEd (Bachelor of Education).

During the last year of my degree, I joined the job hunt along with everyone else but couldn't find a post for IT that I could feasibly commute to. Fortunately I qualified on the Friday and picked up supply teaching from the Monday. I had several supply jobs, some long term, in both primary and secondary schools. During that year I actually got what teaching was about; it all fitted together and just made sense. I realised that I loved being in the classroom and that I had actually found a career that I felt I could be successful in. There was a sense of freedom in supply and that suited me down to the ground.

There was one specific moment that made me realise the power of the teacher and learners working together in an education setting. In a Year 3 class, I had a refugee child who spoke no English. He was lovely and often went out with a Teaching Assistant (TA) for support, but he was always in class for numeracy. I was in the zone, you know; dancing around the room, getting them engaged, doing the whole crazy teacher thing. We were working out areas of shapes and I asked the class to solve the example we had just been through. And there it was: a voice I had never heard, saying the correct answer. It was him, the little refugee boy. The look on his face was magic. In that moment, we met across any cultural or language divide and I knew that something special had happened. It made me realise that education was what I cared about, not necessarily teaching IT. That experience in primary led me to another supply contract, which ended up being my first proper job.

A dream job

That first job is the ideal that I have continued to chase but know I will never find again. It has become a pure and holy image in my head. It was so unique, such an opportunity. The school was brand new, having been an amalgamation of a village's separate infants and juniors and a nearby primary. It was part of Building Schools for the Future and the building had been finished in July ready for the new school to open in September. It was amazingly well resourced with outstanding IT facilities, a sports hall, rainwater toilets and an outside space to die for. But it wasn't all good: the amalgamation had led to redundancies.

That aside, the head's philosophy felt revolutionary with a totally creative approach to learning, including pulling the caretaker and cleaners into the mix. Classrooms became these amazing living projects creating space for learning to develop instead of chalk and talk. Although I didn't know it at the time, it set the foundations for my own vision of education.

For a year it was amazing – and then I screwed the whole thing up and created a situation where the group mentality turned against me as the outsider I was clearly still seen as. In the summer holidays, I had an affair with the deputy head. I was young, she was older, and I was flattered and attracted by the power of it all. I was totally in the wrong; I was definitely mature enough to know that it was not a good idea. The relationship ended amicably but it quickly became complicated when rumours spread; we had clearly been 'seen', even though we had tried to hard to keep it private. The complicating factor was that the deputy head was married to the head. In the end it all came out and the deputy head became the victim – and I the perpetrator. It felt totally unfair and unbalanced.

The group from the primary rallied around her and my position became untenable: some staff refused to talk to me and many requested not to work with me – both hard in a school where all aspects of the day were collaborative! I also became aware that my work was being deliberately sabotaged. I recall one time when I had produced an outline for a fundraising idea which was tied in with creating links with a school in Africa. When I couldn't find my paperwork, I was not too worried: I was often disorganised. Yet nothing prepared me for the surprise of hearing that my plan had been actioned by the SLT – having been presented by the teacher in the classroom next door.

The head was clearly happy I wanted to leave as I was on a permanent contract, and he went above and beyond to secure me a new post. I started at my new school in January.

A school in disarray

The head of my new school had come to my previous school and seen me teach as part of the interview process. She knew how my school had worked and what my teaching style was, so I assumed that part of her reason for choosing me was to do the same thing in her school. I was so positive about starting. It was a fresh start and a new challenge and I felt that in a smaller one-form entry school I would be able to have an impact with the ideas that I had learnt. It was a one-year contract but I was confident that it would become permanent. I had a head full of good ideas – but my naivety had followed me.

The building was old and showed it. It was under-resourced and its size meant that there were only four teachers, two TAs and the head herself. Three weeks in and I realised it was a disaster. The school was a failure and I could not imagine how it would ever change.

The headteacher just seemed to have her priorities all wrong and seemed to be more concerned with being known as the head than leading the school in terms of pupil outcomes. I was in a mixed Year 5/6 class with SATs (Standard Assessment Tests) in a matter of months but there was simply no data to work from. No one knew what the class had been taught and there were no records. Assessments across the whole school came from random places including pound-shop books. Pupils' progress jumped all over the place and no one seemed to be bothered by it apart from me; they all just went through the motions. When I raised my concerns with the head, she just dismissed it all. I had 19% at Level 3 with the rest below in the January and I managed to get 46% at Level 3 by SATs. There was no support from the other teachers either; each classroom was like its own kingdom and you just never met or shared. It was so different from my previous school, just so very uncared about.

I had tried to bring forward my ideas about creativity but the other staff were dismissive of them and the head didn't seem keen: I was the newbie and needed to know my place. Other teachers often reminded me that I had to 'understand how things worked here' before I tried to suggest anything. One helpfully told me that I was 'just a teacher', implying that I had ideas above myself, and that was the realm of the leadership. The philosophy was that you shut your door and worked by yourself. I asked to talk to the head and she invited me to her office. It was the type of office designed to make any visitor feel like a small child as the only seat was a child's chair. When I asked her why she had employed me, knowing how I taught, she told me, 'I needed a male teacher'. That dynamic left me feeling isolated and added to my sense that I had nothing in common with anyone.

The head controlled the school in such a rigid way. She had a list of exactly when each teacher should be having their 30 minutes for lunch and would throw you out of the staffroom if you went over. The fact that you had been making an urgent call to a parent or dealing with an injured pupil mattered not.

Things got worse after SATs. With the pressure off, I tried again to be more creative and for things to be less teacher-led. For a few hours a week, I had a TA who was a local and on the governing body. I asked her to lead a group under my direction, and she point-blank refused. Her job was to hear the kids read and tidy up after art; no more and no less. When I tried to get to the bottom of why she felt that way by encouraging her to share her views, she stormed out of the classroom. The next day, I founded myself suspended for aggression towards the TA. I knew I was trapped. In the end the investigation found nothing against me, but my contract was not going to be renewed. I knew I was seen as maverick; I stood out. I also knew that I was not equipped to deal with the internal politics or the isolation. Leaving felt like such a positive. I quit my job at the end of the summer, preferring to take supply jobs rather than stay for the next term. Again, supply led to another permanent post.

The end of it all

When I was on supply for a teacher off with stress, I should have realised that I had to go in with open eyes. When a permanent post became available because the teacher had left due to stress, I should have declined. But I didn't. I was still chasing that rainbow of my first post, desperate for each new school to be the one. No one mentioned my suspension or the investigation so it felt like another fresh start. It was a larger school in a town and was deemed 'unsatisfactory'. The leadership's way of managing this was to apply layer after layer of pressure. For example, every book for every child had to be marked every day. This included comments, targets and marking in a zillion coloured pens. Staff were up each night until midnight just trying to get through 90–120 books.

The staff were burnt out and utterly destroyed. Through whispered conversations, I found that they were aware that what they were being asked to do was having no impact on learning. I knew that they were coming in exhausted and unable to teach. They lived in fear of the collective power of the SLT so no one spoke up or tried to offer alternatives. The SLT had a blind subscription to the views of the head and could not be approached either.

I knew I had reached an end point. I told the head that I was going to have to leave as it was impossible to do the job. I asked him how he expected teachers to cope with his expectations and his reply was, 'My wife is a teacher and she is up all night planning. That's teaching.'

My final memory is when the school improvement partner came to observe me teach. I knew I was leaving but I wanted to put on the lesson of my life going right back to the lessons I had learnt in my first job. I ran a shop in my maths lesson as the end of a topic to draw all the learning together. The visitor loved it and verbally praised me for what he had seen, calling it 'outstanding'. Yet when the feedback came on the official form (which the head had been involved in) it had been downgraded to 'good'.

I couldn't face being in a classroom again. Not in a school. Even supply teaching held no attraction. Those three schools had destroyed the teacher in me. I would love to be in a classroom again now; I would love to see that magic on children's faces when they understand something for the first time. But I have been out of schools for so long, I doubt I can ever return.

Richard and the toxic school

Richard's first school was not toxic; he freely admits that things only began to go wrong for him due to actions he took. These actions led to the development of some toxic behaviours in others, such as the beginnings of a 'groupthink' mentality towards how he was treated after the relationship ended. Richard constantly reflects upon that first school as the highpoint of his career and holds it as the pinnacle of how education can be. His subsequent experience in two schools which we can deem to be toxic has only added to this sanctification of his first post in his memory.

His second school had three features of a toxic school as outlined in chapter 1:

- **Sinking**

  The staff approach to data collection, or their lack of it, highlights how they were really just doing enough to keep their heads above water. They had been asked for data, and they collected it, but it was only enough to tick the box. Richard, arriving as a young early-career teacher, must have been viewed as a threat to the status quo as he wanted them to go beyond the bare minimum and push themselves out of their comfort zone. This enthusiasm was met with resistance.

- **Bureaucratic**

  Richard's enthusiasm was also counter to the traditional hierarchy within the school. Other teachers reminded him to keep his place and not to get ahead of himself. Richard was to have a fixed role of being a male teacher in a small school; his knowledge, experience and ideas did not factor into this at all. The head controlled the school and, for the time Richard was there, there was no deputy; Richard's post was created when the deputy had moved on. In discussing his concerns with the head, he was ultimately criticising her approach and the running of her school.

- **Individualism**

  Richard's attempts to work collaboratively with staff and change their approach to how they saw their roles within school was not welcomed. The school culture involved each individual teacher running their own classroom in isolation from each other. Richard's many attempts to encourage low-level collaboration were perceived as aggressive. Richard realised that he was constantly battling against a culture which did not value teamwork.

His final school also had three toxic elements:

- **Hothouse**

  The whole school leadership had created a school culture of pressure and blame. Standards were often unachievable and were dictated to staff rather than staff collaborating with leadership. The pressure from leadership was to achieve a 'good' from Ofsted, but they had chosen a course to achieve this without any apparent reflection or evaluation of the progress being made. Richard believes that the leadership was fully aware that the standards were unachievable but continued in the course of action in the belief that this was the only way to prepare for the next inspection.

- **Bureaucratic**

  The school was structured in a traditional and hierarchical way with the headteacher acting as a figurehead and the leadership team disseminating his ideas to staff. Richard felt that the leadership team were blind to the effect they were having on staff; the staff who were away sick with stress were talked of as people unable to cope and not having the right attitude to the job. The deputy was after his own headship and openly explained that this is how he would run his school.

- **Individualism**

  Teachers were expected to follow the directives of the leadership team and complete their individual workload. The lack of time and the focus on each teacher being solely accountable for his or her own classroom meant that there were no opportunities for collaboration; any attempt to work together would mean that the teachers were not meeting the standards set. Richard felt that if he could see the flaws, the SLT should have been able to see them too. But there was an unwillingness to change. Instead he remembers struggling to negotiate access to the hall or other specific school areas, as there was no desire to cooperate between teachers.

Summary

Richard was well aware of his own failings and came across as a highly reflective individual. He knew that he had been naive when entering the teaching profession and that this had led him to make choices which, given his time again, he would not make. He was also aware that his personality, and his passion for education, could come across as being overbearing; he knew he could be a difficult person to work with.

Richard was in the early stage of his career, having only completed his NQT year during his first permanent post. He felt that he would have benefited from ongoing mentoring though the early stages of his career, but the final two schools he worked in were not in a position to offer this, instead seeing him as a qualified teacher, the same as everyone else.

Richard's experience in his first post only added to his awareness that his subsequent jobs felt like toxic environments to work in. Rather than being supported and encouraged, he was expected to just fit in and get on with the job.

Richard remains active in education, although now within the prison service delivering basic qualifications in order to support the rehabilitation of young offenders. His enthusiasm and passion are still present; but underneath is a great deal of sadness and grief over the loss of a career that he knows he could have still been working in if only he had been in schools with a different ethos.

Reflections

Chapter 5 - Brendan's story

In this chapter, Brendan's story reminds me of one of my own toxic situations. A headteacher I once worked with would flit around the corridors troubleshooting on their feet for whoever needed it and wherever they could be heard. As a senior teacher, I was often one of the last to know about what decisions had been made - with key messages sometimes being passed back to me from students.

Despite my experience at the time, I found this very frustrating and the environment gradually started to take its toll on my workload and mental health. In leadership, they say a good leader brings people along with them, rather than walking far ahead and expecting others to follow. In these examples from my own experience of leadership, in a toxic situation, the person at the helm often fails to manage the toxic conversations and behaviours that are taking place around them, allowing individuals to sort out their differences. In my experience, where toxic behaviour does not happen, the headteacher knocks the issue on the head with immediate effect - and in my opinion this is best achieved in an open forum, no matter how uncomfortable the situation.

When individuals find themselves working in a school where, for example, your line manager is displaying toxic behaviours, you may be able to reach a stage where you can start to manage this relationship. For example, have public corridor conversations and reduce the number of occasions where you are left alone with this person. In

> more extreme circumstances when the toxic person understands that they can no longer control you, they will do everything and anything behind the scenes to turn your colleagues against you too. In these situations, relationships and behaviours will start to dominate your day-to-day work and impact on your own performance and mental health. Context is needed, but in this situation, this is my number one piece of advice to any teacher who believes that a situation is being used against them: seek professional support from your union or mental health charities who can offer the help you need. Trust your gut and move quickly.

Brendan's story takes place in special needs schools in the South East of England. Brendan qualified as a teacher in 2003 after training to be a Key Stage 2 specialist. He left teaching in 2012 to work in initial teacher training, where he is currently a senior lecturer within a large university.

I had never met Brendan until the summer of 2017 when we agreed to meet in a London pub close to his home. Brendan had started following me on Twitter due to our shared interest in an SEN group which ran a weekly chat. We had often had brief conversations and had several acquaintances in common although we did not know any of them outside of social media. Brendan had responded quickly to my request for stories and we had several video chats before we arranged to meet. I felt that Brendan needed to build a relationship with me, and to see if he could trust me, before he shared anything of his teaching career.

Our first meeting was a little strained, as I felt that we were dancing around topics: only fleeting references were made to any difficulties he had faced. After that first meeting, I sincerely believed that Brendan would vanish back into the ether and we would return to having a sporadic social media relationship. So I was astounded, as I sat on the tube going back to my parents' house, that he had asked if we could meet again. I had told him at the pub that I was around for several days with no fixed plans as part of our general polite conversation.

So, the next day we met again – this time in a quiet coffee shop closer to his department. Brendan's story came out disjointed and rambling, based around recurring themes rather than a chronological view. He was professionally in a positive place and was able to talk about his past experiences with a degree of separation from the emotions he must have felt at the time. He was analytical, reflective and accepting of the past, yet keen to share his life story – not because he needed to for his own benefit, but purely altruistically.

Background

I didn't always want to be a teacher, but it was there in the background my whole life: my mother was one as was my older sister. Growing up, I wanted to do many things – including being a police dog handler – and every profession had that element of care as a core value. After my history degree, I decided that doing a PGCE was the way forward. There was some expectation from friends that I would apply to be a secondary history teacher but I knew I wanted to work in a special school and doing a primary course seemed the most relevant.

I didn't expect to get a job in a special school straight away and spent my final term on the PGCE applying for what seemed like endless Year 4 jobs. Amazingly, a special needs primary advertised a post that was suitable for NQTs and I had to apply. I was offered the post on a year contract with a view to it becoming permanent once another member of staff retired.

I think that this was my best year ever in teaching. The school was forward thinking and supportive and I found that I was valued – treasured, even – as their first NQT. There were more challenging times – like when my elderly teaching assistant repeatedly undermined me – and times that no training could prepare me for – like when one of my class died due to their medical condition. That was tough. Really tough. I have never attended a more joyous funeral yet I was so unprepared for it. I was in such an adult role but far from being an adult. But I loved that school and always set it as the benchmark for how a school should be. The head was inclusive and made you feel valued and respected, but she ran a very tight ship! The school was such a positive place to work and the staff cared, and loved, the pupils they taught. Life, in all of its rich diversity, was celebrated and valued.

My class were challenging and the learning curve was steep – no PGCE year prepares you for how to change an older child's nappy or how to feed a child through a stomach PEG. It was new, crazy, and utterly wonderful. My sheer joy in seeing a learner with severe profound and multiple learning disabilities (PLMD) respond with a smile to having their hand rubbed; experiences I would never forget I loved it. As the youngest member of staff by nearly a decade, I had a school full of 'work mums' and 'work dads' who wanted to take care of me, protect me, and encourage me in my role. There was a real sense of pride for them in having an NQT, and everyone simple assumed that I was going to be a permanent fixture of the school for many years to come. I did as well.

It all changed at Easter. The funding that they had used to pay for my post was not available and, as there was a drop in numbers, they could not really justify having me. I was gutted, but the school were brilliant at helping me find a new job using all of their local knowledge and contacts. The head was clearly upset at having to let me go and I was heartbroken at seeing my perfect role and school taken away. It felt so unjust and unfair that I had worked so hard, done so well, but was to end up losing out. I had unrealistic hopes that the other teacher would retire or that a last-minute stay of execution would happen with the school finding enough money in the budget to pay my salary. I don't think I accepted that I was truly leaving, even when I had found a new job, until that very last day. Leaving that school was unbelievably hard and I spent the leavers' assembly in tears. My class handed me gifts and I managed to keep my emotions in check until they played a song for the Year 6s.

A dream gone wrong

So, my new school was as close to my first job as you could get on paper and was only a few miles further to travel. The current head was wonderful, savvy and totally in control of the large staff team. Within a week of being employed, the bombshell was dropped that he was retiring and his deputy would be taking over as acting head.

That aside, the first term started well within my class but I felt increasingly lonely. The teachers and non-teaching staff were split into two distinct groups. There were simply tons of non-teaching staff: each class had two or three of them and there were 12 classes. They dominated the staffroom and were a loud group, often very opinionated about how good the teacher in their classroom was – or wasn't. To be honest, they were bitchy and like teenage girls, with one of them always ready with a sarcastic remark about how someone was dressed or laughing at an incident that had happened to them. They were totally dismissive of the teaching staff and often looked down their noses at them with this sense that they were simply better at their jobs. However, at that moment in time, they were not too much of an issue for me as I just kept away from them as much as I could. The sad thing was that the teachers, all female, also kept themselves away from me. I was too new, and too 'male', to be accepted into their established and tight-knit group. Over the weeks I gradually got used to working alone, as that was how every other teacher seemed to work there.

At the end of the autumn term, the dynamic head left and the new head stepped in. You could not have had a different type of person running the school. She was chaotic, made snap decisions and was easily led by others. Staff were intimidated by her and she was so controlling over everything we did. It was like being micromanaged all the time. I found that I got on with her alright but it was not a universal feeling. I was only in my second year of teaching and yet I could see where things were going. It descended into chaos for me and it began with an innocent event where I discovered something about a pupil in my class that I shared with the SLT. One of the members of the SLT had been his teacher the previous year and hadn't picked up on what I had discovered. The head was thrilled and so were the boy's parents. The SLT member was not.

She had been a difficult woman to work for. When I first started she had attempted to befriend me and would share gossip and stories with me. I hadn't wanted any part of it and whilst I remained polite, I didn't fuel her own self-importance. She absolutely rated herself and was a complete extrovert. She wore the most garish clothes and the strongest perfume that left a lingering reminder that she had been in your room long after she had left. The basic undertone was that she was a rising star of the school and would one day lead it so a lot of staff courted favour with her, riding on her coat-tails of success. I had found her irritating and self-absorbed but had kept my head down until this issue with the pupil.

Her revenge started with talking about me to her team, sharing gossip and tittle-tattle, which then spread through the non-teaching staff group. She was party to some knowledge about my personal life as I was going through a difficult time with an ongoing medical issue. I would overhear things being talked about that mentioned some of this yet I had no proof that it had come from that SLT member; it was just a hunch. Then the comments started about my packed lunch. It seems ridiculous that a grown woman was acting like we were pupils at school ourselves – with her being the popular one and me the class nerd – but this is exactly what happened. She would openly tell me that my food looked like vomit and (as it was sometimes done in public) her gang of staff would join in with comments like this. The debates about my packed lunches upset me so much that I increasingly ate alone in my classroom, wishing that I could lock myself in. These types of comments gradually became broader to include criticism of my shirt and tie combinations and my class assemblies. On one occasion I actually saw her smirking when I tripped over in the lunch hall having caught my foot on a pupil's wheelchair. I wanted the ground to swallow me up and it was hard to retain any dignity when you have spilt custard over your trousers! I can joke about it now but at the time it was horrendous. It felt like bullying. No, it was bullying. My confidence and enthusiasm for teaching was gradually being knocked out of me. The lack of male company also began to take its toll; I just didn't fit in anywhere.

I distinctly remember trying to get staff on my side. There was one time when I tried to bribe staff with food. There was an expectation that, on a teacher's birthday, they would provide a buffet for the staffroom. I don't just mean a few cakes, I mean a whole buffet: cheese, crackers, fruit, crisps, drinks and everything else you can imagine. A poor birthday spread could make it hard when it came to directing the support staff in the classroom as it was taken personally – a lack of respect to them, I suppose, due to the difference in salaries and status – and I had seen them make other teachers' lives a misery. I put on the best buffet I could afford – bearing in mind I had just purchased a house, was in my second year of teaching, up to my eyeballs in student debt, and suffering from a long-term medical condition. The party platters of food from a local supermarket were met with a cool response: apparently they were mostly on diets and therefore unable to eat the majority of what I had brought. My meagre buffet was picked at but the majority was left for the cleaning staff to have once we had all left. I cried on the way home. I was a young man who had fallen in and out of love, had my nose broken playing rugby, and had sat with my grandad as he died. Yet I still cried my eyes out about a buffet. It sounds ridiculous but it just shows you how much I wanted to be accepted by them. I knew that I didn't really like them and that my nemesis had ruined any chance of me having any friendships, but I had still wanted them to like me – even just a little bit. All it did was make me continue to feel like an absolute outsider and more lonely than I had ever felt before.

I also tried to get staff to like me by being the most helpful person I could ever be. If you needed the ink changing in your printer,

I would sort it. If you were struggling with a display, I would mount it. I really thought that these small acts of kindness would make them take notice of me. Instead I just ended up getting used without any thanks or credit given to me. This was really apparent when we had our hydrotherapy pool opened by a local celebrity. Doing a display in such a humid environment isn't easy but the head had wanted something up showing how beneficial the resource was for our school. The subject lead for interventions had been chosen to do it as she had a lot of material ready to go up. To prevent it from looking a damp mess, each piece had to be laminated and the wall carefully backed with this thin shimmery plastic that had a life of its own. It was a nightmare and, with a strict deadline, there was no way she would get it done. So I offered to help – and ended up doing most of it, staying late and arriving early even when she hadn't bothered to turn up and help. When the praise came from the head, it was all for her. She said nothing about the work I had done nor the additional display I had up in the corridor leading to the pool. It sounds so petty in hindsight, but at the time it wasn't.

I tried to talk to the head about how I was feeling and how hard I had worked without notice. I was welcomed in and sat down, pouring out the whole saga and listing all the times I felt I had gone beyond my role. It must have seemed so trivial, but all the little experiences had built and built until the dam had burst. I spoke from the depths of my soul, hoping that this might be a catalyst for change. It wasn't. The head did nothing. I had mentioned some of my struggles with particular staff members and the pressures I was under in my personal life, but it was all put back onto my shoulders and became my issue to sort out: I wasn't trying hard enough to join in; I was isolating myself; I was taking jokes to heart. I needed to be stronger, get tougher and stop complaining. I left that office dumbfounded and doubting myself. Was I wrong? Was I imagining it all? The more I thought about it, the more convinced I was that I wasn't wrong – there was something about that school that was very, very wrong. I remember spending hours at home searching for a new job – any job – just to get out of that building. I looked at retraining out of education altogether and thought about becoming a social worker as I felt that my skillset would make it an easy transfer. Thankfully a job in an all-age special school cropped up and I decided to give teaching one last throw of the dice.

The final school

This new school started really well and it felt good to be back in a special school setting where learners seemed to be the focus and the staff looked like a team. The head reminded me of the one at my first school: she was dynamic, caring, and inclusive. She was new to the school but seemed to have quickly gained the respect of those around her even though the former head had apparently been highly regarded and loved. I felt valued and began to get opportunities to access new courses and develop new skills as her approach was so focused on developing all her staff. The immediate colleagues I worked with were supportive and I found teachers of a similar age. There was also an NQT and I felt quite boosted by being able to share the wisdom of my teaching experiences. I probably came across as overbearing but I was just being enthusiastic again. I really felt that I had been right to stay in teaching. I even got a small promotion and took on greater responsibilities in the school, running pastoral groups to support parents with many aspects of having a severely disabled child. I considered applying for promotion in other schools, but I didn't because I just loved being part of a dynamic and exciting school. I simply had no reason to leave and I wouldn't have cared if I had stayed in that role for many, many years.

It all changed dramatically when we had a surprisingly bad Ofsted. It was totally unexpected and the school, which had previously been judged as 'outstanding' (and was happily assuming that that hadn't changed), dropped to 'requires improvement'. I have never experienced a more uncomfortable staff meeting than the one we had the day after the inspection ended. Leading up to it, the mood had been buoyant; and although some texting had gone on the night before (with some insecurities raising their heads), the general assumption was that it was nothing to worry about. Once the news was broken, we were all sworn to secrecy and left to go back to our respective classrooms, trying to come to terms with how different the world might become.

The pressure started with the local authority questioning how such a catastrophe could have happened. The focus became the SLT and there was a mounting pressure for answers to be given. Within a few months, they had all gone, bar the deputy. The head had resigned to become a consultant; one assistant head left for a new post and the other took early retirement. The deputy became acting head and a whole-school restructuring began with fewer SLT posts and a more fluid approach to managing the Key Stages in the school. After a year, a new head was appointed and a second restructuring happened, this time with increased TLR (Teaching and Learning Responsibility) positions. By this time, I was seeking promotion to such a role but nothing cropped up that I could ever apply for; there was always one essential criterion I could not meet and the roles seemed to be targeted at bringing new blood in rather than using the talent already there.

Cracks began to show in the staff team. What had been a supportive school used to team planning and cooperation was gradually forced to split into departments, each fighting with the others for access to resources. Many staff began to leave, as they just didn't like what was happening. I wanted to leave but felt that I ought to stay out of loyalty to the children and their families. I regretted that decision for years. Then another restructuring happened as we amalgamated with a smaller special school nearby. The morale of the staff hit an all-time low, largely because some of 'our' staff had lost out on job roles to some of the new ones joining. Staff were off sick with stress, left the school, left teaching altogether.

The main issue was the new head. We were already dubious about where he had come from and how he was appointed – he was from well out of the area. He felt like an absolute puppet: head in name but actually just a yes-man to those with more power. He rarely left his office, passing on the face-to-face work to the deputy – who people had respected and who I had hoped would be head – and began to get a reputation for being distant, without a clue how to lead and manage a school going through such a crisis. The rumour mill started to churn about us becoming part of a MAT and, lo and behold, that was exactly what happened. We were rebranded and, whilst our head remained, he was under the guidance of an executive head that I simply couldn't abide. It felt like a huge setup.

I saw my role eroded before my eyes: a new member of staff was brought in from another school in the Multi-Academy Trust (MAT) to be my line manager and effectively demote me. Having been used to an environment of praise, I now entered one where those in favour got – and those who weren't didn't. I was not one of the chosen ones; I watched others getting training or promotion over me when I knew that I should have at least had the chance. I would sit in my car and cry – repeatedly cry, feeling stuck and lost. I quizzed my head, who basically said he would support me to get something new but had his hands tied for helping me to achieve anything more if I stayed. There was no way I could stay. My loyalty to the kids and parents had gone. It was all self-survival from then on. Thankfully a former colleague gave me a heads-up about a role at a university teaching about SEN. I went for it and managed to get it. I finally feel valued, appreciated and supported to have a career again after those years of utter dejection and turmoil.

Brendan and the toxic school

Brendan's first school was not toxic. Instead he describes just how positive an environment schools can be for their pupils and staff. The school was high achieving, graded 'outstanding' by Ofsted, and the staff working there were passionate and dedicated. The pupils were at the heart of everything that happened and, off the record, he described numerous events, sometimes attended by celebrities, to fundraise and promote disability awareness in the local community.

His second school had three features of a toxic school as outlined in chapter 1:

- **Balkanisation**

  Brendan's school was one with a clear distinction between teaching and non-teaching staff. The larger group were the non-teachers, which were made up of TAs and a few Higher Level Teaching Assistants (HLTAs) and numbered around 30–40; there were only 12 class-based teachers. The non-teaching staff dominated both formal and informal occasions. Brendan was repeatedly asked to move out of somebody's chair in the staff room and often had his lunch removed from the fridge for breaking the unspoken storage rules. Brendan did not feel that he was accepted by either group.

- **Individualism**

  Brendan's school did not use a collaborative approach to planning, which meant that each teacher planned and made resources in isolation. Often Brendan would be seeking a specific resource that he knew would be effective in his classroom, only to be met with the response that it belonged in somebody else's classroom. Brendan ended up largely purchasing his own resources or borrowing things from people he knew from his PGCE.

- **Groupthink**

  Some of the staff at Brendan's school developed a groupthink approach towards him, following the lead of the SLT member he upset. Staff clearly felt a need to associate themselves with the SLT member of staff; maybe it was due to her position in the school or because she had a dominant personality. Whatever the reason, staff who had previously been friendly became openly hostile. There was only one TA who openly defended Brendan; she was already outside of the non-teaching group because she had refused to get involve with incidents which had occurred prior to Brendan joining the school.

In his third school, Brendan faced five features of a toxic school:

- **High staff turnover**

  Brendan's school had initially been through many years of stability and the staff team was settled. As changes began to happen in the structure of the school (especially in the leadership team), staff began to leave. This included staff who had recently been appointed to the leadership team but left after only a year in post. There was also an added turnover of staff due to the amalgamation with another school and the fact it became part of a MAT. The turnover of staff created instability and meant that roles were constantly being redefined and staff were taking on, or losing, elements of their jobs. Brendan felt that this fluidity of responsibilities was confusing for staff and pupils alike and meant that it was hard to have a long-term vision due to constant change.

- **Sinking**

  Over the years that Brendan worked there, the school gradually began to sink. In his final years, the culture was one of 'turn up, teach, go home', with staff detached from their roles to such an extent that there was no willingness to do anything extra to support even the most vulnerable of pupils. Many teachers were working to rule, which, in a large special school catering for pupils with complex needs, made life challenging. An example Brendan gives is when the school was faced with a viral infection spreading through the pupils, leading to an increase in nappy changes until the situation was brought under control. Although changing nappies was not part of the teachers' roles, to Brendan it was crucial to support the non-teaching staff in coping with the situation at hand. Brendan was in the minority amongst teachers; the majority refused to take part in any additional intimate care that pupils needed.

- **Repeated restructuring**

  Numerous changes in the leadership and nature of the school led to changes within the whole school structure. No restructuring ever quite seemed to work, nor had the chance to embed before other factors came into play. The emotional impact of both the amalgamation and the move to becoming a MAT was never addressed and many staff, like Brendan, became frustrated that their skills were overlooked. At a classroom level, Brendan mentioned that staff went through several changes to their practice which were never fully embedded. The school effectively ran two different systems inherited from the two amalgamated schools. This led to confusion as staff ended up using the approaches of the school they had originally been employed by. This naturally caused problems with pupils moving between teachers from the different backgrounds.

- **Bureaucratic**

  By the time Brendan left, the executive head was running a hierarchical system where those not in a leadership position had little chance of involvement in developing the school and sharing their ideas. The school head was the figurehead but often spent more time out of the building than in it due to the role including responsibilities across the whole MAT. When he was there, he was distant from the pupils, leaving the day-to-day running of the school to the deputy. This frequently meant that decisions were not made in a timely manner as so many depended upon the head being present. This included decisions that they felt the deputy should have been able to make, such as agreeing to leave of absence requests, but nothing happened without the head's agreement. The tight bureaucratic system meant that staff often had little personal autonomy over their practice and any requests for training or resources often took too long to organise – with the result that many staff stopped trying.

- **Balkanisation**

  Brendan's only criticism of the school when he first arrived was that the Key Stages were very distinct and separate from each other. This separation was largely due to the school site, which had several different buildings with post-16 in a separate provision on the other side of the town. As the school culture changed, the gaps in the staff team grew with the splits occurring in each building. Brendan felt that he was becoming increasingly isolated and felt that his teaching was affected due to a lack of any stimulation from colleagues. These splits became worse when the amalgamation took place as there was little attempt to unite the workforce as one school. Although the divisions lessened over the years, many staff only socialised with those that they had known under the former structure.

Summary

Brendan presented as an individual finally at peace with education after spending the majority of his career working in toxic environments. Although he remains passionate about education, he has no desire to ever work as a teacher within a school again and would certainly never seek to work in leadership.

He was very new to teaching when he encountered his first toxic school and struggled to cope. He felt that he was treated as a teacher in a place of great knowledge and authority – and not one who had only recently qualified. Brendan felt that the chaos in his personal life made it harder to cope with what was happening in his professional world. Although he didn't wish to go into details, he did seek medical help and spent some time taking antidepressants.

Brendan felt that it was pure determination and self-belief that keep him going; he has often thought about how different life might have been if he had got a permanent post in his first school. This school was the highlight of his career in teaching, although he is aware that there is a danger of idealising his time there.

Reflections

Chapter 6 - Gwen's story

What is striking about the story in this chapter is that Gwen is a seasoned teacher. Experience is a very important factor in teaching, yet regardless of length of service, anyone working in a school may find themselves in a difficult situation at any point of an academic year. This can happen to the best of us, newly qualified or those in leadership.

As we read in this chapter, difficulties do present themselves to those with experience; for example, teachers who become expensive to employ or when milestones in life make teaching a harder career choice - becoming a homeowner; starting a family; working part-time.

With wisdom or changes in our personal lives, experienced teachers learn to opt out of long working days for family and health reasons, or simply because they have learnt how to deal with the job in hand, despite the accountability system goalposts shifting.

Anyone reading this chapter can take something away, and what resonates from the experiences cited in this chapter is that relationships must be in place for teachers and schools to achieve a collective good. This will only apply to you if your school values relationships and contributions to society above examination performance.

Gwen's story takes place in mainstream schools in the South West of England. Gwen qualified as a teacher in 1999 after completing a secondary PGCE in performing arts with a specialism in dance. She continues to work as a teacher and is currently part-time in the final school she discusses.

Gwen and I had discussed her feelings on education several times on Twitter but had started to talk about them in more depth in 2017. Our shared connection was based on the high levels of SEMH needs in her current setting. She showed interest in sharing her story and had initially wanted to discuss her current job, but through our conversation she realised that her previous experiences were also relevant to her feelings on education. This was due to the contrast with her current school.

Our first meeting felt like it was setting the scene. On several occasions she said, 'That will be important later.' By the end of that first chat, we had only just started to discuss the first school that she felt was toxic. The going had been slow, largely due to the fact that she had buried a lot of her feelings very deeply over the years since she had worked at her current school. Having to reengage with those feelings, to recall the pain, was challenging and unsettling. She also found the whole concept of talking about herself in such detail almost embarrassing. After an hour we drew our conversation to a close. A friend she had agreed to meet up with arrived early and I felt that this was actually fortunate timing for Gwen: the tricky experiences had not yet been shared. I was expecting Gwen to disappear into cyberspace, never to be heard from again.

This was not the case and we arranged a second time to chat. Due to distance, we largely communicated through video calls and online messaging systems. The rest of Gwen's story flowed with more ease and she seemed more confident to speak her mind even though some of the events were very fresh and raw.

Background

I had wanted to be a dance teacher since I was 11 and started secondary school. Our dance teacher was amazing and such an inspiration that I couldn't imagine wanting to do any other job. She was so full of life and vitality and brought the best out of us. I'd had a tough time in primary school and was academically behind in maths and English by the time I moved into secondary school. Fortunately my parents were able to pay for extra tuition so that I achieved the grades I needed at GCSE and A level to go to university. I got a BA (Bachelor of Arts) in Performing Arts, but by that time I was engaged and my focus was on getting married and buying a house so I didn't do a PCGE until a few years after I had graduated. I had also had a wobble after graduation about whether I could cope with teaching teenagers; but the desire to teach overcame any initial fears.

My PGCE placements were so important in forming me as a teacher. They instilled in me a desire to see pupils in a holistic manner but also prepared me for (what I thought was) the worst that the profession could throw at me.

My first teaching practice was in a very traditional school with a dusty old guy heading the performing arts department. It was old-fashioned teaching with lessons scrawled on a piece of A4 paper and his own unique notation for dance steps. The kids loved me. I was young and into the music that they were into, so they experienced street dance and hip-hop, which was revolutionary in the school. I suppose I was seen as radically different from what they knew. I felt I could do the job and that I was going to be a great teacher and really inspire kids. The confidence of youth that I suppose every trainee feels at some point.

The second placement was the absolute opposite and almost ended in disaster. It was another more-traditional setting but with a head of department who was a bit of a battle-axe, and I always felt that I wasn't meeting the grade. I began to experience a sense of hopelessness and I really felt that I couldn't do it anymore; I was simply not cut out to be a teacher. It got to the point where my husband actually came to the school with me to talk to the head as he was so concerned about the effect on my personal life. There we found the head of department nearly in tears worrying that I was going to quit teaching when she felt that I had such potential. So I stuck with it. I realised how crucial experience would be in my career – and I would have handled the whole situation differently if I had been able to draw on my own knowledge and experience – but accepted that it would take time to get to that place. I learnt a lot about myself and it refined the values I had started with. I knew that pastoral care – for both the kids and staff – was important. I genuinely felt that this rocky patch was something that I had got over and wouldn't face again. Why would I? I would be entering into the profession with more confidence, self-awareness and experience. I would be prepared.

The world of teaching

My first job was in a properly posh school. It was a grammar school with a unique difference of having a sort of added-on hub for traveller children in the grounds that was run by the local authority. They rented the building, I suppose. This was unique to the local authority and several schools had a hub attached so that the traveller children could attend a school close to where they were living at that time. As the school was pretty rural it must have made sense for them to negotiate a deal. It just showed me how cool the school philosophy was! The rest of the school had all the trappings you would imagine, from a house system and prefects to academic gowns. The school encouraged pupils to take a lead and therefore they organised their own music, dance, and sports competitions. The whole ethos was healthy competition, with staff in a supporting – not leading – role.

My line manager was fantastic, as were the whole leadership team. It was a very open school and staff at every level were encouraged to get involved in the running of the school. If you had an idea then you knew you would be listened to and you would be supported. This meant that we had a degree of freedom in running school trips or setting up events or special days. Teaching here was a dream. The children were respectful and conscientious and I felt that my professional knowledge was valued. It wasn't an easy job by any means as the level of ability was so high and the need for challenge was crucial. Yet I coped and it seemed that my thoughts at the end of my PGCE were validated: I had been able to succeed in teaching and was actually enjoying myself. This is exactly what I had imagined teaching would be like.

Career break

Life continued in this way for several years. I felt that I had progressed as a teacher and had started to think that one day I would like to take on a leadership role. When I was pregnant with my first child, I decided to go part-time. The school was very supportive of this and, at the time, I felt that I would return to full-time teaching in the near future. I enjoyed the balance; but when I felt that I wanted a second baby, I decided to leave – after five wonderful years – to be a stay-at-home mum. My husband was also a teacher and I knew that we would find it hard to raise our children and both work full-time. I also knew that it was a profession which I could return to in the future, so taking a career break didn't seem like the end of the world. In fact, teaching seemed like the perfect career for a woman with young children. I knew I was a good teacher and I was certain that I would find a job when I was ready to return to work. I didn't regret leaving at the time, but in hindsight I was arrogant and had taken that school for granted. At that point, I just didn't realise how lucky I was to work in that school; and I was naive in thinking that this experience was a reflection of every teaching job. I felt that I had given five years of myself to the job and that I could bank that experience and cash it in when I wanted to return to work, like I would somehow be in professional credit after my career break.

My plan had been to take five or six years out until both my children were more independent. I felt that this would give me the chance to ensure that they had a good start to life but also not leave me too long out of teaching so that I was able to get back into the swing of it when I wanted to. Things took a turn for the worse at home and we hit a financial crisis when my husband was made redundant after his school was merged with another. He got some money from the whole situation and he did find another job, but it was not the assistant head role he had previously. So after two years at home, I knew that I had to find a new job, and quickly – I couldn't afford to be picky. I wasn't worried at this point. I was still in the firm belief that I was a good teacher and that I knew how schools worked.

Not a mirror image

I saw a job advertised in a different local authority but close enough to home and thought I had landed on my feet. It was similar to my first job, had a history of amazing performing arts productions, and the interview had gone really well. Although I was only applying for a second-in-department post, I was assured that I was to have the majority of my week teaching dance with some lessons of drama. I was also informed that there would be an opportunity for me to apply to be head of the performing arts department within a year. This seemed ideal. I would have time to get back into full-time teaching and find my feet before taking on the leadership role I had wanted to secure. They appointed two of us on that day: me and an NQT. I spent my summer holidays writing all of the schemes of work (so that I could hit the ground running) and generally preparing myself for a new venture. My initial worries about leaving the children were balanced by a genuine excitement about returning to teaching.

On my first day there, I received my timetable to find that I was not teaching dance at all. I was gobsmacked and assumed that there was a mistake. There wasn't. Instead of dance, I was teaching a mixture of drama, PSHE and some PE. Meanwhile the NQT had nearly a full dance timetable; I was told that this was necessary for her to complete her NQT year. It was also made clear to me that the opportunity to be a head of department was out of the question. I was never given a reason why, but it was clear that the rigid structure of the school, in terms of the staffing and levels of leadership, meant that there was simply no room for my role to exist. I felt that I had been completely mis-sold the job. I spoke to my line manager, my head of department, but the matter was not taken any higher and I had no way of doing that myself. I was so frustrated. Surely they must have known when they appointed us that I wouldn't actually be teaching dance? I felt that they tried to placate me about the whole thing by giving me the responsibility of mentoring the NQT. Looking back, this was an utterly stupid decision: I had been out of full-time teaching for over two years, I had no experience of working in the school, wasn't even teaching the same subject as she was. Yet somehow I was magically going to support this young teacher.

I soon began to realise that, because I wasn't teaching dance, it was hard to mentor the NQT beyond handing over all of the planning I had lovingly produced. I had little support from my line manager, had no idea how to line-manage an NQT, and was constantly behind as I hadn't had the chance to prepare for the subjects I was expected to teach. I was stuck in the middle between the NQT and my line manager. Stuck. I began to feel quite dejected; I was watching someone else teach the subject I was so passionate about. I began to realise that I wasn't important enough, valued enough, to matter to those on the SLT. I was a lowly teacher in an unimportant subject. I was childcare rather than a professional.

The problems were not just within the department I worked in. The school was arranged in separate blocks for each department. This meant that departments didn't mix and there was no feeling of community as I had experienced in my first school. Whole-school events were limited and had to be driven by individual teachers rather than supported from the top down. Even charity days were not valued or supported although leadership were happy to take credit when they felt like it. There was a huge gulf between teachers and the SLT, with the Middle Leadership Team (MLT) passing messages down from on high but not taking anything back the other way.

The lack of community combined with the isolation I already felt; the situation was awful. I can remember so many occasions when I drove home crying, sat in the bath crying, and went to bed crying. Although money was tight, I couldn't take full-time work there anymore. I put a request in to go part-time, using the excuse that my baby was less than a year old. I desperately wanted to be at home; but there was a part of me that didn't want to be beaten by this profession and still believed that I was a good teacher at heart.

I hated my job. I hated that I felt so alone and that the school culture seemed to encourage this. I hated not feeling part of something. I knew from my first job how positive schools could be and I wanted to experience that again. So when an old colleague told me of a new post at another school in the town, I arranged to meet the head of department at a gig to see if we could get along. Thankfully, we did – and I handed in my notice after only a year in the school.

Felt like home

My new school felt like a homecoming. It wasn't as traditional as my first post but it had the same ethos of being like a large unruly extended family. The staffroom was always heaving and there was an active school social life.

My line manager was the best model for leadership I have ever had. He was supportive yet challenging; he was led by a desire to see our pupils grow into young adults; he was protective of his department and fought for us when he needed to. The head was one of those old-school types that you don't really see anymore. He had been at the school for over 30 years and he knew the parents and grandparents of our pupils. He was a local man and heavily involved in charity events like the annual hot air balloon festival. He was an absolute character and was able to deal with challenging kids and parents by taking an almost fatherly approach to leadership. He didn't have children of his own and openly said that the kids at school were his kids. He would appear in classrooms and join in with lessons and say things like, 'What do you think of Miss? I employed, her you know. Isn't she a great teacher?' The school was brilliant.

Yet it had to end. When he retired, the deputy head became the head. He had worked closely with the old head and basically tried to replicate what had gone on before. But it didn't work. The skill of the old head was in the extensive relationships he had and, in hindsight, a lot of what he did may have frustrated staff if they had known about it – but we didn't know as we were not involved in it. The old head dealt with stuff, supported us and ensured that the pupils respected us. The new head conducted the business of the school in a really open way, often leaving staff feeling undermined. When you repeatedly see a pupil who has been bullying younger pupils sat in the breakfast bar with a member of the SLT, drinking coke and eating a bacon sarnie, smirking at his peers, that makes you feel like a fool. It began to cause a rift between us and the pupils. A rift which exists to this day – the pupils rule the school. We had a restructuring and in their wisdom the number of SLT posts increased. This was utterly pointless as there were so many people at that level and not enough at the middle leadership levels working on the shop floor. Then we had another restructure and the departments were all reorganised, with an SLT member running a 'theme', as they call them. I am in the arts theme now but I was previously part of dance and drama. The pastoral team also vanished into the SEND (Special Educational Needs and Disability) theme with the loss of the year pastoral leads. This means that no one knows these kids any more and there are no staff to offer them the support they need.

Now we have the worst behaviour I have ever seen and the lowest staff morale ever. Staff will go home sick at lunchtime rather than face an afternoon constantly firefighting issues. The new head doesn't show any interest in us as staff. He doesn't value the kids or praise them. This is a really challenging socio-economic area and the kids come to school to feel cared for. Now it's a case of permanently excluding them. All of the extracurricular activities that staff led have gone as no one sees the point in going above and beyond any more. There are only a handful of us in the staffroom because the restructuring created work zones where staff were encouraged to spend their breaks and eat. That whole joy of chatting to colleagues with totally different perspectives has gone.

Each term sees the introduction of a new marking system, behaviour policy, or some other fad that we are expected to follow, lest we get pulled up in lesson observations. Everything is a gimmick but we are expected to comply and the pressure is immense. The danger is that you will forget to do one of them; that mistake of not mentioning the 'Word of the Week' in a lesson when the SLT are in could cost you your job.

I had nine months off for my third baby and, on my return, it had deteriorated even more. I decided to go part-time and that is the only way I am coping; if I was here full-time I would be on the sick. Family pressures are harder to deal with when your whole day is stressful and exhausting. I know my husband gets the brunt of it. I know my baby does too. Every day is survival. I left work on Friday and cried all the way home as the situation just feels so helpless and my career so pointless. My family are watching me go through hell, having to support me to keep myself together and trying to keep me sane and well. That isn't teaching. That isn't what I joined this profession for. And we are now facing another restructuring in January with 20 more posts going. I am actually praying that my job gets cut as I can use the payoff money to go to university and retrain. If I could walk out today, I would.

Gwen and the toxic school

Like Richard's and Brendan's first schools, Gwen's first school was not toxic. Her narrative is filled with positivity and passion for her first post after some challenging experiences as part of her PGCE. The school was creative, well led, and a positive environment for both the pupils and the staff. Gwen had begun to realise that she could be the teacher she knew she was inside.

Her second school had two features of a toxic school as outlined in chapter 1:

- **Bureaucratic**

  Gwen's school was highly structured with a clear departmental system. For reasons she never knew, the post she had applied for did not materialise – probably largely due to the fact that it did not fit into the way the school was organised. She found it hard to challenge this as her only means of raising concerns was through her line manager, who was head of department; she was unable to go around this person and discuss it with anyone else. She also found herself struggling to support the NQT in the department alongside managing her own workload; but, again, she had no avenue of support other than trying to raise concerns through her line manager. She felt that the structure created a one-way system for passing information: it only seemed effective for passing information from the top down.

- **Balkanisation**

  Gwen's school had been built in such a way that each department had its own block. This meant that she felt isolated within her department and had little contact with any other teaching staff. For someone who was clearly unhappy and struggling, this only served to compound her negative feelings. It also appeared to create issues for the school regarding its ability to function as a united force because there was little sense of a genuine school community.

In her third school, Gwen faced two features of a toxic school:

- **Repeated restructuring**

  Gwen's school continues to repeatedly restructure after the retirement of the initial leader. Each subsequent reorganisation changes an element of the school but has a knock-on effect on staff morale as well as on the sustainability of certain posts. This has meant that Gwen has not felt secure in her role and is uncertain about the future. She has started a new school year unsure if her own department will exist by the end of the summer term. She is actively seeking employment in another school whilst she works out if she wants to remain in teaching.

- **Hothouse**

  Gwen's third school moved from celebrating the success of individual teachers to trying to move towards a uniform and corporate approach to teaching. Each lesson follows a set format and there are key strategies, words, and actions that every teacher must be seen to do in every lesson. In a setting where staff are already anxious about their jobs, this only adds to the pressure and does nothing to raise the standard of teaching and learning. There was no staff consultation on these new approaches to teaching and learning and Gwen feels that they have no way of challenging the system. Staff who do not follow the prescribed system are highlighted through observation – with a repeated failure to comply leading to disciplinary action.

Summary

Gwen was a passionate teacher who was willing to give one more school a try before she gave up on education altogether. Her only fear was not surviving with her health and wellbeing intact long enough to get out of the school and find a new post.

Gwen is not an early career teacher. She is a teacher with extensive classroom experience and knowledge and is full of ideas for how to continue to create positive learning experiences. This is something that her school should be valuing as a resource rather than attempting to force her to fit into a mould so that the staff team ends up bland and uniform. Her uniqueness as a teacher is undervalued and her relationship with the pupils is seen as irrelevant.

Like Brendan, Gwen is in danger of romanticising her first teaching post. She is aware of this, and whilst she does think about the past, she is a woman with her eyes set firmly on the future.

Reflections

Chapter 7 - Jessica's story

In my career, I have had limited experience of working in pupil referral units (PRUs); but over the past decade, I have been exposed to them through my leadership career managing exclusions, behaviour and sometimes crime. Working in some of these institutions training the teachers, you can get a good sense of what a challenge it must be to work with students at the brink of permanent exclusion, perhaps facing prison and dealing with very challenging situations at home.

If I said a pupil referral unit was a high-stakes environment, this could quite easily be read as an understatement in some of the most challenging PRUs across the country. I can only imagine how difficult it must be for an individual working in a PRU to sustain a positive outlook and manage their own mental health. As a school leader, I do understand how complex it is to manage not only your own wellbeing, but that of all the teachers that you are working with. It amazes me that this pressurised environment can translate into creating a toxic culture. Surely we should be trying to achieve the complete opposite?

In this chapter you will learn that collective teacher efficacy has the greatest impact on student outcomes. Meaning, if you choose to work in a school alongside other colleagues, then the agreement should be that you are all working towards the same goals. It takes just one kink in the chain to break this common goal, and if there is one person who

> greets their colleague's professional wisdom with cynicism, and this is actively promoted in public, you can understand why we are losing good teachers to the profession – even if pregnancy is one means of escape!

Jessica's story takes place in mainstream and alternative provision schools in London. Jessica qualified as a teacher in 2006 after completing a primary PGCE. She continues to work as a teacher.

Jessica and I had interacted several times on Twitter due to a shared interest in SEMH (Social, Emotinoal and Mental Heath) learners. Over a few months, conversations drifted to discuss how we felt working in alternative provision and we began to share some of our experiences. From here, I asked Jessica if she would share her story in full and we arranged to meet.

Meeting was challenging, as she was a very busy mum to two children under five. Our first meeting was in a play centre in Kentish Town during the summer holidays. It was not ideal, so rather than using it for Jessica to share her story, we instead used the time to get to know each other as we had never met face to face. It was good to meet someone who understood the world I worked in and I hoped that this would make Jessica feel comfortable enough to share her story at a later date. When the announcement came for the end of her children's allocated play session, we finished our first meeting and made an agreement that we would continue our discussions by email.

After several months of silence, Jessica suddenly emailed with the first part of her story. The second part followed in quick succession, with Jessica explaining that she had taken so long to respond due to the fact that she had not felt ready to engage with her past in case it affected her ability to maintain her professionalism in her current role. It felt to me that Jessica had tried to use her previous experiences to create a positive identity for herself and to learn from the experiences so that she did not repeat the mistakes she had seen others make. Jessica had a fragile and emotional side to her very clinical persona. I was left wondering about the extent to which she had coped with the challenges in her career by ensuring that any setbacks drove her harder to succeed.

Background

Although I had a dream of going to university, I worked as a classroom assistant at a primary school after sixth form college to buy myself some time to think and hope that I would work out what I wanted to do with my life. The school was a small mainstream one and I spent most of my time in the Reception class. The teacher was much older than I was, probably close to retirement, and I felt that she talked down to me more than she encouraged me. I was confident and used my initiative but she probably saw this as a challenge to her control of the classroom and I never felt accepted by her. In her eyes, I was there to set equipment up, wash paint pots, and sort out children who had wet themselves in assembly. I survived the year although, at this stage, I never thought about teaching. Instead it inspired me to take an interest in people and cultures.

I ended up studying sociology and it was only during my final year that I decided to apply for a PGCE due to an experience I had on placement in a CAMHS (Child Adolescent & Mental Health Service) Tier 4 setting for young people who had serious mental health needs. I was running a small project with Key Stage 2 pupils who were resident in the unit, and I knew then that these were the kids I wanted to be with. I was impressed with how the staff at the unit worked with the children, how they tried to build relationships, encourage small steps of change, and saw them as being able to lead a fulfilling life. It was an immensely stressful environment and I witnessed some children in crisis to an extreme I never thought possible.

During my PGCE I had two placements at schools which were in deprived boroughs. I saw children with similar backgrounds to those in the unit and found the placements immensely rewarding. Both the schools had ambitious staff who both supported and encouraged me. I felt increasingly confident that I was on the right track and decided to look for a post in a similar area.

First teaching post

In hindsight, pulling up to a school for an interview where there were young children sat on the roof was probably a sign that the job I was applying for was in a school that was struggling. The school had been through a very difficult Ofsted and they were therefore subject to a lot of pressure from the local authority. The borough had some areas of high socio-economic needs and many of the 'nicer' families were opting to attend a primary school just down the road. It was made clear from the start that the school was employing people to raise standards and I was one of several NQTs they had appointed. It was only once I had started that I realised that the school had repeatedly brought in new staff because no one seemed to want to stay.

My role was in Year 4. It was a hard year and the pressure was intense without any let up in the pace. I learnt a lot in that school that I still use now, but it was very difficult and I was often marking books until midnight and ensuring my planning was always the best it could be. This was on top of the work I had to do for my NQT year. At times I questioned if it was really worth teaching; nobody seemed to care that we were NQTs and had only been teaching for five minutes. The consultants working with the school treated us the same as they did the staff who had been through the Ofsted – sometimes more harshly – and I felt that the pressures placed on the SLT found an easy outlet on those of us at the bottom of the system. Towards the end of the year I was told my temporary contract wouldn't be renewed due to the falling pupil numbers, and I began to hunt for a new post.

Moving on

I still had not been put off working in tougher socio-economic areas as I was able to see that I might simply have ended up in a 'bad' school. I ended up teaching Year 6 in a challenging area a considerable commute away. I had applied for the Year 4 job but someone must have recognised something in me so I entered a new world of SATs and the additional pressure that they brought. I worked in Year 6 for nearly three years. I loved it and enjoyed watching children succeed. The school was well organised with clear systems and procedures and the staff team were supportive. The school was vibrant and forward thinking. The SLT saw the value in upskilling staff and investing time and money in them; staff wanted to stay and so the investment paid off. It was a large school so there was a parallel class to mine that was taught by the deputy head. We got on really well and we shared planning and resources, meaning that there was some let up in the pressure I had felt before. He also helped me outside of school hours and I felt that we had a positive and trusting relationship.

The pressure to achieve the best outcomes for my Year 6 was huge. Yet this was nothing compared to the pressure of what Year 6 school data could do for the league tables. This pressure – and that of being successful in the next Ofsted – dominated my life. I loved it, but I also missed out on so much that my non-teaching friends did. I could never do the spur-of-the-moment evening drinks for a birthday or know in advance that I could definitely see the latest film at the cinema on Sunday. Teaching was all-consuming and I envied some of my friends who had greater freedom in their careers for a similar wage. Yet I did enjoy it largely because I felt that I was supported and valued in my role.

Moving out of mainstream

My father became ill and this made me realise I needed to be working closer to home. The commute was taking its toll as well: I was often spending up to three hours a day travelling on the bus and tube. A family friend worked in an alternative provision school in my home borough and had always told me that I would love working in her school as the hours gave you a better work:life balance and I would get some additional money in a SEN point. The deputy head I had worked with tried to talk me out of it, telling me that moving into such a school would have a detrimental effect on my career; but after visiting the school, I decided to apply and I took up post in the summer term as a Key Stage 2/3 teacher.

Once I had started my new post, I quickly realised that alternative provision was very different from mainstream. There seemed to be a culture of 'containment' and worksheets and low expectations. I remember looking around at my colleagues in a staff meeting and feeling like Miss Honey in a room full of Miss Trunchbulls. I had worked with challenging pupils in all of my previous roles and I knew that high expectations worked. But it was difficult to come into a school as a new teacher full of enthusiasm when the more experienced staff had been in alternative provision for many years – and most had been in that school for the majority of their careers. To some staff, I was young, a woman, primary trained, and with no alternative provision or secondary experience. In their eyes, I had a lot to learn.

Fortunately, a few staff seemed interested in my ideas. Whilst this was good, it also concerned me that so many of them seemed unaware of strategies that were common in mainstream education – and a lot of them had not had any recent CPD (Continuing Professional Development). As my time at the school moved on, I began to experience success in my classroom by using a primary teaching model with low-ability and low-confidence learners. This began to filter through into other classes and the headteacher supported me (to a degree) in delivering regular CPD and looking at the type of curriculum we offered.

Whilst many were sceptical, there was one teacher who was hostile towards me. In public she would nod and smile but she refused to try any new ideas. This was in part due to the school culture, which was one where individual staff did their own thing with a lack of overall cohesion; joint planning or sharing your own good practice was greeted with cynicism. There was also a lack of motivation, from staff like her, to want to change. Having worked in mainstream, I knew that there was simply more time in alternative provision to get the job done; yet I was surrounded by a team who didn't appear to have any commitment to their job or any desire to do anything more than the bare minimum. There was simply a lack of aspiration both for themselves and the children.

On a personal level, I was frustrated as I was being paid significantly less than the other teachers. They were all receiving two SEN points whereas I was only awarded one. I believed that I was often working harder – and to a higher standard – than others, as well as taking on leadership responsibilities. After a few months, and some conversations with my family, I decided to discuss this with the headteacher. She was expecting me to take on some 'serious' leadership tasks before I could achieve the extra pay. I was young, naive, and inexperienced and I accepted her at her word. I eventually achieved a second SEN point, but not without increasingly long working hours and a job role that seemed bigger than other staff on the same pay grade.

All was not as it seemed

This was the beginning of my gradual retreat from working in that school. It had opened my eyes to the possibility that all was not as it seemed and I began to notice it everywhere. It became apparent that the headteacher was out of her depth. One day, standing in her office, I noticed that there was the usual bookcase with a wall of smartly labelled files. The usual suspects were there: Health and Safety, Performance Management, Key Stage 2 SATs Data etc. There must have been about 20 files sat proudly on the shelf. The headteacher had left the room, so, being inquisitive, I wandered over, stood on my tiptoes and peeked over the top of the spines. Every file was empty. There was not a scrap of paper to be seen.

I was concerned but relatively alone and therefore only had my family to reply upon. Talking with them, more and more odd things stood out and I wondered why no one had ever questioned them before. Like the fact that resources frequently went missing and needed replacing. Not just small things – the odd printer and a rug or two disappeared as well. People just seemed to accept it. But it was so bizarre. So, there I was. Ambitious in a school with just a veneer of a functioning workplace. I knew I would have to look for promotion elsewhere. Yet the world changed before I was able to take that step.

I arrived into work one morning to be faced with a frantic-looking secretary and two women in sharp business suits as if they were part of the FBI – they just lacked sunglasses. As I was processing the novelty of this clearly unplanned event, the headteacher walked out of her office accompanied by a smartly dressed man. He walked with her straight past me and out of the building. I was gobsmacked and turned to the remaining visitors. They were talking to the secretary; she eventually turned to me and asked me to find the deputy and assistant heads. I scuttled off to find them and garbled some incoherent message to them and we all returned to reception. The two women greeted them and invited them into the head's office. I was left outside. Although I knew something serious was up, I slipped into the only routine I knew and went to my classroom. Within a short space of time, we were all called into the hall. Here we sat on chairs whist the two suited women informed us that our school was closed for the day – parents and taxis had already been called – and that we were to assist in any way which we were asked. Our headteacher and the business manager had been formally suspended. Five staff names were then called, including mine, and we were invited to a separate meeting where we were informed that we were effectively a temporary SLT who would be running the school.

Over the next few months, as the investigations progressed, this SLT tried to pull together to not only keep the school functioning but also to try to make progress. But relationships began to fray, with splits becoming visible between those who supported the headteacher and some of us who had begun to question if we should keep things as they were when this was an opportunity to head in a new direction. It was around this time that I began to feel more and more isolated. A close colleague achieved a promotion and I began to dream that I could find something in the school he had moved to. The gossip and negativity spiralled out of control when he left and, at times, it felt like some staff were bullying others. I certainly felt like this was happening to me. Things became worse when the headteacher retuned to post. Those who had clearly stood beside her during her absence were in her favour, whereas those of us (myself included) who had seen things differently were given the cold shoulder and actively excluded from being involved with the running of the school. I was thankful that I fell pregnant during this period and I was looking forward to maternity leave, electing to take the full 12 months. Being away was bliss, especially because the colleague who had left for promotion made contact to inform me of a post with a TLR attached. I applied and got the job. Returning to school and handing in my notice was the best feeling possible so I left to join the Key Stage 2/3 PRU in the summer term.

A fresh start

Although the job was tough, I now felt supported and valued. One of the deputy heads (my former colleague) and the headteacher were friendly and encouraged me to contribute to defining the ethos of the school, and I had freedom so long as I reported back to them on a regular basis. I was working in Key Stage 3, got along with the other teacher, and was able to develop my coaching skills with her. The support staff were equally hardworking and proactive and it felt like a genuine Key Stage 3 team.

The only stumbling block was the other deputy head. For reasons I never knew, she really disliked me and made this fact clear. Whilst she publicly nodded at my suggestions, she was quick to dismiss them to the rest of the SLT in private. I felt constantly undermined and had to persevere to represent myself in the way that I wished others to view me.

But otherwise, life was pretty good and, during this time, I had a second child. It was a struggle balancing two small children and full-time work and I only managed it with the support of my partner and parents.

I thought this was a school I could really progress in and I eventually became assistant head. I knew the head was as ambitious as I was; when he left for a new role, I was gutted. As we were a split site, the other deputy became the acting head. Her animosity towards me became more noticeable as she progressed into her new role and began to establish herself. She was ambitious too but in a self-serving way, to the extent that she didn't care whom she trod on to make herself known. Rather than having the freedom and encouragement to progress, I found my ideas either dismissed or ignored until they suddenly reappeared in a slightly different format as her own. No one knew how much I resented her or how upset she made me feel – with the exception of my former colleague who I opened up to in part. For the most part, I internalised my feelings, cried in the car on the way home, cried to my husband, and then stuck my chin up and carried on the next day.

It is really hard to admit but I did feel bullied by her, yet it was so subtle and elusive that I could never evidence how I felt. Even if I could, what would I say and whom would I say it to? It was largely little off-hand comments which I knew were aimed at me but were said in such a general way. For example, I had always dressed very smartly in dresses and jackets but had only really ever worn flats as I found them comfortable – and better suited to working in a PRU when you never knew if you were suddenly going to have to sprint anywhere! When I had become an assistant head, I had continued to wear them as I had a full teaching timetable. The acting head passed a comment in an SLT meeting about professional dress, specifically mentioning how flats did not give off the same air of professionalism in meetings as a smart set of heels. It sounds silly saying it as it sounds like nothing, but it was comments like this that I faced on a daily basis and they felt personal. Really personal.

I was caught between the proverbial rock and hard place. I loved the school so much and I had a fantastic teaching assistant who was proactive and reliable. I felt comfortable with my own teaching and had made some really good contacts in the wider

London area due to my previous head promoting my work to others. I knew I had begun to have an impact on teaching and felt that there was so much more that I could achieve if I was only given the chance. Accepting that this time had ended was very hard but I just couldn't see myself staying in that school anymore, being belittled on a daily basis.

All that glitters

I saw an assistant head post advertised for a PRU in a neighbouring borough. The post was a new one for the school and was part of an ongoing restructuring that seemed to have been going on forever. Whilst it was a significant pay rise, I was saddened that there was no teaching commitment with the role as the main focus was managing the Key Stage 3 unit and leading on pastoral and safeguarding across the Key Stage 1–4 provision. I was excited by the challenge and had really felt a connection with some of the SLT when I had been interviewed. We seemed to be of a similar mindset and I could really see myself fitting in. The deputy was older than I was but seemed laid back. She was quite bohemian in dress and style and had hair tinged with pink. She led on teaching and learning. The head was more formal, very much the business type: more a manager than a leader, really, and always dressed in sharp suits. He was late to teaching (having previously worked for the police) and definitely had a corporate management approach. He was very influential – the kind of person you did not say 'no' to. There was then a leadership team of sorts made up of an assistant head for the primary, an assistant head for the medical unit, and the business manager. It was a large setting based on one sprawling site and the majority of staff had been there for many, many years.

When I started in the September, I was full of hope and enthusiasm. I was ready to put the past few difficult years behind me and commit myself to a new challenge. Within a matter of weeks I realised that everything I had thought about the school was wrong and that, aside from a new job focus and more pay, I was heading backwards, not forwards. It started when I tried to implement some changes in the pastoral side of the school. In the interview, I had shared my vision for the setting in revisioning the pastoral staff into outreach and early intervention roles instead of being as school-focused as they were. So, when I started the job, I began to formalise this into a policy and a restructuring plan for the staff it involved. When I came to share this with the head, it was met with a lukewarm response. Whilst he agreed to look at it, his main focus was on timetabling and micromanaging staff.

Whilst I knew I couldn't act on anything major with the pastoral staff, I knew I could start to address their performance management and CPD needs. The staff had previously been managed by the deputy but it became apparent that they had pretty much been left to run themselves and make their own decisions and had free rein to really do as they pleased. I soon felt a sense of resentment from them at the fact that I was putting systems in place to monitor and evaluate the impact they were having in the school – and especially their effectiveness in supporting parents by running groups and networks. My enthusiasm was met with passive faces and often downright rudeness. When I met with them to share some new paperwork, some staff actually walked out of the meeting. I turned to the deputy and head for support, but rather than having them back me up, my concerns were met with shoulder shrugs and patronising suggestions about rethinking my emotional intelligence.

This sort of event happened on a weekly basis. I would ask staff to hand their timesheets in and I would get nothing from them. I would analyse the data from the work they were doing with families and share it with the SLT to have it glanced at and put in the back of a folder. Time and again I asked the head for his suggestions about my policy ideas and he repeatedly fobbed me off or asked me to focus on working on the timetable. I realised that no one in the SLT really respected me and this became glaringly apparent when decisions were made without my involvement; on several occasions, huge changes to the school were announced in SLT, which the head and the deputy had worked on together. I felt like an outsider: I didn't fit into the SLT as they were all supportive of the head in speaking out against me either to my face or behind closed doors; I didn't fit into the teaching team as I wasn't teaching and they largely seemed to adore the deputy anyway; and the pastoral staff hadn't accepted me either and would turn to the other deputy for clarification of things I had asked them to do. I was virtually alone.

Amidst all of this, my father died. It made me question what I really wanted out of life and I decided that this was just not it. I don't recall much of the time after his death but I don't feel I was supported through it beyond being given a few weeks away from work. I think I got a card, but the fact I don't remember just shows that I had given up caring. I longed to return to mainstream but became increasingly paranoid that this would never happen.

I managed to survive the year only because a secondment opportunity arose for school I am now in – thankfully back in mainstream where I feel happier. I think the head knew that things were not working out as planned and he was very supportive in helping me secure the position. Initially it was for a year, due to the MAT being newly formed; but by Christmas it had become a permanent vacancy, so I applied – and was successful. It is a tough role in a challenging socio-economic environment but it feels like I have come full circle. Not everyone likes me, I am sure, but I have learnt to live with that. The difference is that there are plenty who do and I have the full backing of the SLT.

Jessica and the toxic school

Jessica's first school had three features of a toxic school as discussed in chapter 1:

- **Hothouse**

  Jessica's school was a highly pressurised environment due to the school struggling to keep pupil numbers up because of its reputation.

The team of consultants working with the SLT brought in many new initiatives and changes, often in rapid succession.

- **High staff turnover**

  The school's reputation and the increased external pressure put on staff meant that many people chose to leave, often midway through the year. This created a lack of stability for those working there and meant that there was not a foundation for the school improvements to be built upon.

- **Bureaucratic**

  To Jessica, the SLT seemed to be trying very hard to take control of a school that was in chaos. They did this through tightening up the hierarchy with pressure from the consultants trickling down to become intense pressure on the staff at the bottom of the school. It was a school where everyone had a set and fixed place. As an NQT, Jessica felt she was trapped in a box.

In her third school, Jessica experienced four features of a toxic school:

- **Sinking**

  Jessica's school had low staff turnover. The majority of staff had worked in the setting for a significant amount of time and there was a lack of personal drive by staff, which Jessica felt impacted on their enthusiasm for securing the best outcomes for their learners. Staff were comfortable in the roles they had and did not welcome change or challenge to their existing practice. This was seen in all levels of the school, with the headteacher also showing a similar lack of professionalism. This resulted in the investigation into the running of the school.

- **Restructuring**

  Jessica's school had been restructured just before her arrival and had to be quickly restructured again when the headteacher was suspended. This placed immense pressure on the SLT in particular and made many staff like Jessica feel insecure as there was a lack of direction in the way that the school was heading, especially in creating the culture and ethos of the setting. The return of the headteacher then caused a third restructuring as she returned to post and staff like Jessica were moved out of roles.

- **Individualism**

  The school encouraged teachers working alone and in relative isolation. The fact that many staff were long-standing members of the school contributed to this: they were set in a comfortable pattern where they were happy to work alone. Jessica felt there was no real desire for personal progress.

- **Groupthink**

  The sudden changes in the school due to the investigation led to the development of a groupthink mentality among those who actively supported the head in opposition to those who were trying to make progress in a different way. The return of the head created a clear dividing line between those who were favoured and those who were not. Many of the staff had initially been supportive of using the space created by the head's absence to bring in some small elements of change, but Jessica felt that they capitulated when the head returned and put their own beliefs to one side in order to be accepted by the larger group.

Jessica's fourth school is interesting as, for the majority of the time she was there, she would never have said that it was a toxic environment. She was happy, felt like she was achieving, and had no desire to leave. Yet one change – the deputy taking on the acting head role – changed everything. This highlights how quickly schools can become toxic and that, in some cases, one toxic element can be catastrophic for those working there:

- **Bureaucratic**

  The promotion of the deputy to acting head changed Jessica's school experience from one of collaboration to a more bureaucratic style of leadership. Jessica felt that the acting head wanted to establish herself with a view to applying for the role on a permanent basis. As we discussed in chapter 1, when bureaucratic schools fail to represent the knowledge and needs of those within them, problems can arise – and this is what Jessica's experience was. From feeling like a valued member of a team, she began to feel excluded. Due to this move towards bureaucracy, Jessica's position as assistant head meant that she was constantly reminded by other SLT members that her outlook should be focusing on those below her and passing down information from the head rather than seeing her role as collaborating with others in a leadership position on a more equal footing.

Jessica's fifth school had four elements associated with a toxic school environment:

- **Restructuring**

  Jessica joined the school during a long and challenging restructuring which had initially been caused by retirements and promotions of some of the previous post-holders as well as the expansion of the PRU due to increased pupil numbers. This restructuring had been going on for several years by the time Jessica arrived. This had led to some staff feeling quite demoralised, with others openly hostile as they had disagreed with some of the appointments made.

- **Sinking**

  Although there had been a new intake of staff due to expansion, the majority of staff had been in the provision for over a decade. There was a lack of motivation or willingness to change and any new initiatives were treated with cynicism. Jessica found that most staff would ignore her requests, often making personal appeals to the other deputy or the head to get permission to be excluded from completing tasks Jessica had asked them to complete. It seemed that most people working there were stuck in a rut they hated but were unwilling to change.

- **Bureaucratic**

  The school had a very hierarchical structure which the restructuring was further cementing. Jessica had worked with some staff who were not part of the leadership team but were enthusiastic and thoughtful. Jessica wanted to promote some of their ideas to the deputy and the head but they were largely dismissed because they had come from the lower structures of the school and not from the leadership team itself. Conversely, ideas promoted by the leadership team were generally accepted even if they were not appropriate to the setting or well thought through. The confidence of the head meant that many followed his ideas without question.

- **Balkanisation**

  Although the school was on a single site, there were clear departmental boundaries, each headed by a member of the SLT. This meant that the primary, Key Stage 3, Key Stage 4, and medical unit staff generally only mixed with the other staff in their departments. Whole-school staff meetings and activities were rare and there was no communication between subject leads across the departments.

Summary

Jessica's career in teaching has been dominated by toxic experiences. In some cases these were short lived and largely due to unplanned-for changes in the settings. However, some of the schools had been toxic environments for a considerable amount of time.

Jessica appeared to be a resilient and determined woman who was not prepared to let her previous experiences ruin a career she loved. She had never thought about leaving the profession, instead aiming to learn from what she had seen and ensure that she became a leader who would run a school that was free from toxicity.

In her role in mainstream, she is experiencing her first opportunity in a supportive SLT as a senior leader and is aiming for headship. This has not been easy and, from our conversations, it is clear that there are elements of a toxic school in her current setting. However, Jessica is aware of the needs of her staff and has a plan for addressing any support needs they might have.

Reflections

Chapter 8 – Martyn's story

Even if you are second-in-command, choose to work in a challenging school and it could be the end of your career. In Martyn's story I am reminded of a recent toxic situation that led to me leaving my place of work for a second time. Now in this situation, I am not talking about my headteacher being toxic, but the system itself.

I could never visit another person's school and tell you how good it is within a one-day visit. Never. So, why do we believe our inspection system is any more reliable? With a little bit of training? Machine learning or data analysis to make ourselves understand the complex world of learning and an individual student's achievements?

Teachers are now working within a system where they have to demonstrate progress and provide evidence for the past academic year to prove their worth. And the stakes are raised when a visitor attends the school with high authority and expects this to be on the table when asked.

It is my belief that the root cause of the toxic culture living and breathing within our schools lies at the very top of our accountability system. There are a large group of senior people working within our education system who believe in the validity and reliability of how we measure success. Some are rewarded for their success: given bonuses funded by the taxpayer; asked to take on failing schools under the pretence of, 'We'll do a better job'; perhaps even awarded a 'gong' for doing so!

If we truly want a world-class education system, we need to remove the metrics from teaching. This can quite easily be achieved by doing two things: abandoning the Department for Education's league table system – I've yet to meet one parent (who is not a teacher) who understands them; and rapidly reforming the school inspection process, thereby moving from the high-stakes accountability of a one-day inspection to a broader understanding of the complex work that takes place in schools – beyond data. I could be delusional. I do believe we need school inspection and I do believe schools and school leaders should be held to account. But there are other ways of achieving success without it breeding toxicity.

Research published by National Foundation for Educational Research (NFER) in September 2018 asked 'What is the impact of different models of accountability in education on curriculum, standards, and teacher and pupil engagement and what factors affect this?'

The research mapped the main features of accountability systems for primary education in 13 international jurisdictions. The NFER's analysis yielded recommendations relevant to relationships between accountability and the core topics of interest: curriculum, standards and teacher and pupil engagement.

The 'literature suggests that how accountability measures are implemented can affect the extent to which there is confidence in standards'. Several jurisdictions with less accountability in reporting to the public are, according to the Organisation for Economic Co-operation and Development (OECD), achieving better outcomes.

Martyn's story takes place in one school where the experience was so dramatic that he ended up leaving the profession. It highlights the fact that whilst a school may not have many toxic factors, one or two can be enough to affect staff. Martyn qualified as a teacher on the Graduate Teacher Programme (GTP), having had previous careers in youth work and as a school-based mentor working with pupils at risk of exclusion from school. He continues to work in the broader world of education, teaching part-time on an ITT course and spending the rest of his week working for an education charity.

I met Martyn through Twitter in 2017, although we didn't actually meet in person until I attended the same conference as he did in 2018. I remember following his account as we seemed to share a similar educational philosophy and I was going through a spate of following people who worked in ITT. Although we had exchanged a few comments and had taken part in a range of debates in common, our interactions were pretty innocuous. In September 2017, Martyn posted a tweet about how schools had a responsibility for taking better care of their staff and that he could still have been teaching if his school had viewed this as a priority. Through a private chat, he discussed his feelings further and decided he wanted to share his story. Martyn and I didn't meet face to face to talk, nor did we speak via a video link. Instead he shared his story by email, which meant several to-and-fro messages between us to clarify points or for me to ask questions to draw out more of his narrative.

What was clear from the start was that Martyn, like Richard, retained a real passion for teaching. He was someone I could imagine keeping pupils enthralled, having the ability to tell a good tale. Yet here was a man who, in spite of his clear belief in the value of education and the impact a teacher can have on pupil's lives, was outside of the classroom and removed from a job he had loved. The saddest part for me as an outsider was the feeling that, in a different setting, Martyn would have flourished and thrived. Sadly, his only teaching experience is set to be his last teaching experience and the profession is surely darker for not hearing his gentle Welsh tones in the classroom.

Background

I grew up in a council estate in North Wales in the 1980s. My family were financially poor but we were well supported and loved. My parents valued education and would have been happy for me to do anything I enjoyed, be that leaving school at 16 or going to university. Although home was happy, the surrounding picture was not as joyful. Whilst the miners' strikes were far to the south, they affected us all, as many people saw our country being torn limb from limb by a government hundreds of miles away. Life was no easier in the north. By the time I was born, the mills were in decline; the first shut in 1977. By the time I was 10, the mills were all gone and the estate I lived on was full of unemployed people who had only ever known working in one job their entire lives. At the time I didn't know what was happening. As an adult I knew I had witnessed the devastating impact of deregulation and privatisation on communities that had once been so strong and so meaningful.

My childhood was challenging and I sometimes found myself in trouble with the police. It was a common story of underage drinking, although I was once arrested and charged with handling stolen goods. What I can say is that I was one of many pulled into that way of life. I knew that education was my way out, that it could be emancipatory and transforming. Like any kid, I had good times and bad times at school. I got into the usual trouble for not listening or for being silly. Certainly nothing as serious as I was involved in outside of school! There is one teacher who stands out: Mr Garron, who taught me history and politics. His influence on my thinking has continued to this day and he inspired me to see university as a real option for me and not just a pipe dream for a working-class boy.

University opened up so many opportunities for me, which is why I left home and chose careers that were working directly with young people. Not every job was great. Many were awful with poor pay or limited chances for progression. I have done everything from youth work to being a school mentor. It was this last non-teaching job working with kids at risk of permanent exclusion that cemented my desire to be a teacher. These were young people on the brink. Some of them had challenging families; some of them had got mixed up in the wrong crowds and got carried away. Regardless of their starting point, they were all on the verge of being kicked out and it was my job to try to maintain their relationship with their school. It didn't always work out, and sometimes I felt that I had failed completely; but I felt I could do so much more – help so much more – if I was a teacher.

Going onto a GTP course didn't faze me. I chose history, as this had been a growing passion since Mr Garron taught me. My first placement school was the one I had been a mentor in so it was familiar and supportive, if a little strange to be on the other side of the ropes! It was a tough school in a challenging area and I loved it with a passion. My other placement was the exact opposite, being a middle-class school in a leafy suburb. I had a perfectly fine time but it confirmed to me that my heart was in schools that were challenging, and that really helped me to narrow down my list of schools that I was going to apply for a post in.

The first and last post

By the May of my GTP year I had found what I hoped was the first of many teaching roles. The school was a large comprehensive in a similar area to that which I had grown up in as it was in an area of high deprivation. The headteacher was really approachable and I was made to feel very welcome. He was an old-school head, close to retirement, who was a people person and leader above being a manager. In hindsight he had not coped well with the pressures being heaped on schools and his paperwork and record-keeping was shambolic. Yet that didn't matter to me as an NQT: he was someone who loved education, had made time to get to know the pupils I taught, and valued other staff. He supported my ambition and in my second year I became assistant head of year. In the next two years, I again took promotions, finally becoming head of department in my fourth year. The department was small – just the four of us – but we all got on well and I was confident that we would continue to develop.

This was when things took a turn for the worse: the headteacher retired. It was a sad time but not unexpected. His last assembly in the autumn term was poignant. After Christmas, our deputy became acting head and then head by the end of the spring term. There was no gradual change with him; we seemed to jump straight from an era of self-determination to one of hyper-accountability and micromanagement. As a new head of department, I felt swamped. My role seemed to have doubled. What I can recall is that there was an expectation to:

- complete weekly RAG (red, amber, green) monitoring of pupils with strategies put in place for any pupils not 'safe' to get their predicted levels.
- write arbitrary targets; for example, a GCSE cohort with high grade predictions (A*–C) of 53% were given a 80% target based on nothing other than 'high expectations'.
- change end of Key Stage 3 levels to improve school data. This was still done by teacher assessment in Wales and I felt incredibly uncomfortable as I knew that I was falsifying the data and fundamentally being asked to lie by another professional.
- attend an ever-increasing number of meetings, many of which would focus on data – both how to present it and how to improve it.
- make our performance management targets linked to pupil outcomes; for example, 'to ensure that GCSE pupils get at least 60% A*–C'. These were then used in pay reviews. This was at a time when there was also a reduction in staffing levels and budget, which meant that targets were getting higher and harder to achieve as resources were depleting.

I was not the only member of staff who disliked the way that the school had developed. I cannot say that it was a perfect environment before – I certainly had issues with some elements of practice before the new head – but after he was appointed there was a distinct change in ethos which had turned away from the positive one we had previously known. It certainly became a place where the sense of being part of a collective community vanished and staff began to exist within their own spheres and departments. I was aware that I had begun to become more insular and not be as active in the life of the school as I had previously been.

Life was challenging. I was married with two very young children and was becoming desperately unhappy at work. This had naturally begun to affect my life at home, and it seemed inevitable that there would come a point where something had to give. After three years of running the department, I was diagnosed with work-related stress and depression. I did take some time off with stress – only a week, but that was largely because the local authority I was in had good access to occupational therapy and I was able to access that support quickly. My actual school were largely indifferent towards my mental health needs. They were not overly supportive but they were not totally dismissive either. I can remember having a meeting with the head when I told him that I had been diagnosed with depression. His response was 'Have you tried to exercise?' I don't think he was being deliberately obstructive; he was just not a people person, more of a manager than a leader.

It was at this point that I decided to leave the profession. I had been looking at other options over many months and had seen an opportunity for a funded PhD with a teaching commitment in ITT. I resigned in May by writing a letter to the head. He did try to convince me to stay on and rethink my decision but the passion and desire had gone. I knew it was unsustainable and that I had just been getting through the last few years rather than developing or achieving. I knew in myself that I had to leave – or end up on long-term sick leave and all of the additional stresses and worries that it would bring. Thankfully now I get to work with trainee teachers, many of whom are working in much better schools with excellent leadership. It was a huge pay cut and certainly wasn't a decision I took lightly with two small children to provide for. But it was a better choice than the alternative.

In a recent inspection report the school was graded unsatisfactory across all areas, with weak leadership being highlighted as one of the significant flaws. Although I didn't experience it myself, I am aware of a number of colleagues who were bullied by senior members of staff, with two teachers going to a tribunal. Behaviour in the school was also very challenging. This is mainly because the school lacked consistency and a positive culture for behaviour and relationships.

Martyn and the toxic school

Martyn's single school experience is important as it highlights just how much of an impact the change in school leader can have on the whole ethos of a setting. Whilst his school only had two features of a toxic school as discussed in chapter 1, the impact of these on a confident and experienced teacher was dramatic:

- **Hothouse**

  The new head brought in a lot of sweeping reforms and changes to the way that staff were expected to report on pupil progress. Martyn felt that this was often data for data's sake and did not add anything to the school. The need to show progress also meant that there was an expectation that teachers showed increased progress during Key Stage 3 by reporting that pupils had met a specific level when this had not been the case. These changes brought with them increased pressures on time and workload.

- **Bureaucratic**

  As a comprehensive, the school already had a highly bureaucratic structure with a defined SLT and heads of department in MLT positions. The changes to school leadership further enshrined these principles and placed increasing pressure on the hierarchical structure with decisions made by the head filtering down through the structure. As a head of department, Martyn was responsible for ensuring that the staff he managed were also complying with the new expectations and was, in turn, passing the pressure he was under onto others.

Summary

We cannot know for certain what Martyn's career would have been like if the new head had been a different person or approached school improvement in a different way. We do not know the personal story of the headteacher, his ideals or philosophy; yet research has indicated that the pressures of working in urban schools can influence how headteachers lead and manage (Rayner, 2014). The role of leadership in toxic schools is something we will discuss further in chapter 10.

What we do know is that Martyn was an enthusiastic teacher who could have had a whole career in front of him and chosen to leave, if he wanted to, at a time that was right for both himself and his family. Instead he left teaching abruptly making a choice which, although he does not regret the possibilities it has created, has clearly had lasting emotional and financial consequences.

Bibliography

Rayner, S. (2014) 'Playing by the rules? The professional values of head teachers tested by the changing policy context', *Management in Education* 28 (2) pp. 38–43.

Reflections

Chapter 9 – Coping as a teacher in a toxic school: the eight characteristics

Helen offers a wide range of ideas in this chapter – especially the hallmarks of a toxic school. She shares how teachers can keep their heads above water in a sinking school, how we can remind ourselves of our values and pedagogy when times are challenging, and what we need to do – and how to take a step back – when we spot the signs.

If I could offer just one idea that significantly changed my professional work when times have been tough, is to use social media for professional purposes. Social media has changed the way the world lives and works. In an educational context, teachers are creating, connecting, supporting and learning in and out of school hours beyond the usual classroom experience.

Social connections with educators around the world have allowed hundreds of thousands of people (me included) to get out of their silo to seek support and critique – faster than a conversation with someone in the office next door! This connection provides many benefits: reassurance to those who seek private counsel; an opportunity to receive or provide coaching and mentoring; support when most needed; and so forth.

> Using social media has changed my professional life beyond all expectations. Most importantly, in toxic situations it has allowed me to connect – for free – to a wider professional learning network on my terms when I've needed it. No contract; no obligations to take part; no preconceived ideas; but countless professional connections. You would be surprised how many hundreds of thousands of teachers are on social media sharing ideas and supporting one another through their online relationships.
>
> Social connections are something positive for us all; and whether you find them online or offline, they are an important aspect of working relationships in schools. Furthermore, they can help prevent high turnover, damaged mental health and increased workload – as well as the development of a toxic culture.

In this chapter we return to the eight characteristics discussed in chapter 1 and see how you can cope with them – and investigate how the five teachers did. We will also makes links to wider research on school culture and cultural change.

High staff turnover

A school which has a constant turnover of staff is unsettling for those who remain working there for two reasons: staff relationships and continuity. It is hard to develop meaningful and supportive relationships with colleagues if your immediate support network is in a constant state of flux. We all need time to form relationships and learn to trust, and that is difficult to do when it feels you are starting all over again each successive year. The solution to this is to develop relationships with a broader range of people both in and out of school.

Within school there are people other than teachers. It sounds obvious, but we often forget the wider school culture which we work within. You may have a range of learning support staff, administrators, librarians, cleaners, and site managers. Developing a relationship with this wider school network can have several potential advantages:

- Firstly, it can make you evaluate whether your emotional response to your job is shared by others. I don't mean that you go and actively question staff; instead you will learn over time how others feel about and view the school, seeing it from a different perspective. This knowledge can help you decide whether you want to move on to a new challenge or stay and work through what is happening.
- Secondly, these relationships will give you access to positive experiences that might make your time at work something you are able to cope with better. The best 'non-teacher' friendship I had was with a school caretaker. We chatted every morning for the seven years we worked together. His life story was fascinating and I slowly learnt about his family, dreams, and opinions. He also had numerous stories of the school from the past, right back into the Victorian establishment of the place. I looked forward to those morning chats and was saddened when he eventually retired.
- Finally, these relationships are valuable in their own right. Everyone who works in the school is part of the school culture and should be valued and respected. In developing the relationship, you might actually be supporting someone else to feel included and part of the structure as well.

The second issue mentioned was continuity. There is often no continuity with ideas as initiatives are being constantly brought in and then seen to fail because there is no one to drive and embed them. The constant shifting of ideas outside of your classroom is out of your control, but you can keep you own routines and standards. Even if the third marking and planning schemes are in chaos because the changes have been too rapid, you can stick to the practice which you know is successful and works. Even if there is no clear idea on what standard of uniform is acceptable, you can stick to your expectations. Don't get me wrong, this is not ideal. Ultimately the school culture should be shared by everyone, but we are not thinking about an ideal school.

Gwen's story highlighted so much of this. Her way of coping was to maintain the standards which she had and that the learners expected within her lessons. They knew where they stood with her and responded well to the routine, safety, and predictability that she offered. Whilst the rest of the school appeared to be in chaos, Gwen knew that she was providing the best teaching she could in the circumstances, developing her own practice so that she could one day leave and take all of that knowledge and learning with her.

A 'sinking' school

It is easy to feel stuck in a sinking school. The low staff turnover and lack of new initiatives and learning can make it feel like a very stagnant place to be. Watching your colleagues arriving just before the first lesson bell and leaving as soon as they can at the end of the day is hard, and you can feel tempted to be drawn in with the attitude, 'If they can do it, so can I.' Don't.

The reason is this: once you have started to act in the way they do, you will find it harder to motivate yourself enough to make any decisions about your own future. If you have already started to follow their lead then it is not too late to turn back. Make a mental list of everything that frustrates you about your colleagues' practice and behaviour. Do they let the learners down by not setting enough challenge? Do they not engage with new research and initiatives? Do they not model the behaviour they expect from their classes? Keep these in mind and recall why you wanted to be a teacher in the first place. Coping in a sinking school is about keeping that dream alive and finding ways to see the bigger picture. Your school may not offer you any relevant CPD or trial new concepts but you can. CDP doesn't have to be expensive and much is offered through unions and teaching networks. Social media in particular has a lot to offer teachers looking for fresh ideas or ways of finding interesting people to engage and discuss education with.

Keeping your head above water in a sinking school is not easy but it is achievable. The benefits to those who chose to do so are positive. You can keep yourself mentally challenged and stimulated, develop your own practice to form a portfolio of evidence for possible interviews, and it gives you a chance to put your school in perspective by being more aware of the bigger education picture.

Jessica spent many years in a sinking school doing just this. She signed up to emails from education institutes so that she got links to new research or interesting education books. She also developed and trialled her own materials within her classes and built a large portfolio of evidence which she was able to take to interview and to showcase her own teaching style and talent. She turned the sinking school experience into a positive, finding that she had space to be creative and develop as a practitioner because she was free from any external pressure to be doing anything else.

A 'hothouse' school

These schools are the kind where you feel you hardly get time to breathe, let alone engage with developing yourself as a practitioner or trying to make decisions about your future. It is easy to get caught up in the constant chaos and stress and lose sight of your own teaching philosophy. What you need to do is find ways to take a step back.

Taking a step back to reflect doesn't have to take up too much of the time that you already feel is slipping through your fingers. It's about making space and seeing that as being worthwhile and valuable in itself. Ways of creating these short moments of calm and reflection will vary from individual to individual but could include the following:

- Have your break in your teaching room by yourself a few times a week and think about the tasks your SLT have asked you do. Do they fit in with your philosophy? How would you approach it differently if you were in a position of leadership? Have you been given any reason for handing in a comment book with your planning or triple mounting every piece of work on display? What are your SLT trying to achieve by asking you to attend sporting competitions and termly Parent-Teacher Association (PTA) bake sales?
- Use your daily commute as reflection or relaxation time. Download podcasts – education ones on topics you are interested in, learn a language, practise your X Factor audition piece. Just don't use that commute to get anxious about your day; use it to unwind.

- Develop some mutually beneficial friendships with colleagues. If your colleague has the knack of laminating without leaving a trail of creases that looks like a snail has had a party, see if you can exchange your laminating for something you are more competent in but they struggle with.
- Set a time limit to get your marking done and then reset the timer to have a few minutes' break once you are finished.
- Keep a learning journal.

Richard had a hothouse experience and coped by prioritising what he had to do on a daily basis. Hothouse schools make it very easy to fall into the habit of seeing every expectation as being as crucial as the next. One way of evaluating what is important is to use what is either called Eisenhower's Principle or The Time Management Matrix. The basic concept is to split your tasks into four quadrants:

1. **Urgent/important** – safeguarding, some calls/emails, contacting parents, work with a close deadline, problems
2. **Urgent/not important** – some calls/emails, admin tasks, some meetings
3. **Not urgent/important** – planning, making, professional development, staff relationships
4. **Not urgent/not important** – perfectionism, over analysis, some emails

If you write your tasks on post-it notes and draw your grid out, you can move the tasks between quadrants as you feel necessary. If you don't have the space or privacy to do this then you can easily make an electronic version that you can access from your desktop. It is a great visual way of being able to evaluate the pressures you face and prevent that feeling of being overwhelmed.

Repeated restructuring

This can leave staff with many of the same feelings as a sinking school and the ways we can cope are similar. It is unsettling to be faced with constant change, especially when you have only just got used to the last structure and systems. It is natural to fear the new structure, mourn that which you had before, or feel unwilling to engage with what you are presented with and expected to embed.

How you can cope is by trying to distance yourself from those parts which you cannot control and focus on the elements which you can. It can be useful to try to make and categorise different parts of your role into two simple columns: 'in control' and 'out of control'. Things out of your control might include:

- who your line manager is.
- what the vision of the school is.
- whole-school systems for behaviour management.

What you *can* control is your own personal practice and philosophy. This is what I think of as our own *Braveheart* moment. In the 1995 film, Mel Gibson's William Wallace says, 'They may take our lives, but they'll never take our freedom!'

- Firstly, constant changes in the structure of the school do not need to take away your freedom to be the best teacher you can be; the rest of it, the trappings and systems, will always remain secondary to that. Keep to your own routines, including the times which you arrive and leave, how you set out your classroom, and the basics of what you eat for lunch. This focus on keeping your own structures strong can help when those external to your classroom seem to be in chaos and gives you some stability to be the teacher you know you are.
- Secondly, don't get sucked into rumour-based discussions with colleagues; instead, try to work with facts rather than speculation. This will help to reduce anxiety and again maintain your stability.
- Thirdly, look for ways to use the restructuring to your own advantage. There may be scope to further your own career through spotting a gap which you can fill, or initiating a new system; a school in chaos can be a great place to be creative and get experience.

- Finally, talk to people outside of work and get a different perspective. It is easy to feel like you are being battered and unable to act but talking to someone outside of the chaos can help you to see a way through or to put your restructuring into perspective.

Brendan experienced repeated restructuring and found that his way of coping was to focus on what he wanted out of his own career and an evaluation of his own educational philosophy. For him that meant looking at what qualifications he needed to get involved in initial teacher education so that he was ready to take other opportunities when they became available. Like Jessica, who realised that mainstream education was where she ultimately felt she wanted to be, Brendan took advantage of the surrounding chaos to focus on his own goals and aspirations.

Bureaucratic

A bureaucratic school can be stifling especially if you are an enthusiastic practitioner. These type of schools have very rigid boxes which staff are put in and don't recognise that leadership can take place at any level of the school, or value the voices of the teachers who work in them. As discussed in chapter 1, bureaucratic schools can work well for some teachers when their own careers or values are in full alignment with where they work. Yet, for many teachers, this is not the case and these are the staff who can feel that the system is oppressive.

Trying to fight against the weight of the system is futile: you will only expend your energy and run the risk of burning out. Yet, this does not mean that there is nothing you can do.

- Firstly, get to know the school structure inside-out. Watch how it functions and where there may be any weaknesses. A weak spot sounds like a negative but instead can be seen as a place of opportunity. Just as in a school facing repeated restructuring, there are often voids that need to be filled. In a bureaucratic school, this is due to the fact that a rigid system often doesn't match the needs of learners, especially when it is a model which has been imported from a different school. Making a suggestion to SLT might seem daunting, but a well-organised business plan will help, so it pays to be observant and do a little research. Getting involved in something new can make you feel like you are part of the school, develop yourself, and help you to have some control over your career.

- Secondly, you will not be the only member of staff who feels frustrated working in such a rigid school system. Finding other people who feel like you do is a way of getting support. Often, bureaucratic schools can make staff feel uneasy about being too vocal against the system for fear of being ostracised. It is also the case that there may be limited chances for them to share their voice; a staff questionnaire for Ofsted which is emailed to you with your name and role pre-filled for you, and a member of admin staff ready to track you down if your form is not returned, is not teacher voice. Yet, we are human and we do let our feelings show at times. So watch out for those staff who roll their eyes in a staff meeting, doodle on a pad whilst the SLT are delivering the next initiative, or those who bend the staff dress code without actually breaking it. Here you may find some kindred spirits.

Gwen ended up working in a very bureaucratic school with a system imported direct from another setting. She had to learn to accept that there were things that she could not change, and instead focused on turning things on their heads and looking for positives in the chaos. She valued learner comments towards her teaching and repeatedly proposed ideas to her line manager with the hope that she could exploit a gap in the system.

Balkanisation

Schools which experience balkanisation have distinct groups. These may be status groups (as seen in Brendan's experiences with teachers and learning support staff) or subject-group relationships including a possible split into academic and technical subjects. Many large secondary schools have a distinct department set up and it is not necessarily wrong as you can have strong departments and not work in a balkanised school. Where it is challenging for staff is if the structure is rigid, where staff are left isolated (such as Jessica experienced) or where other groups are seen as a threat to the one you are in.

The challenge for teachers is that we work in an age of decreasing school funding and the need to justify every penny which is spent. This can mean that different groups in schools are actively competing not only for finances but also often for the attention of the SLT. Coping is all about trying to work together towards a common purpose (Hargreaves, 2001). This may sound like a big task, and it is ultimately something which needs to be driven by the SLT, but there are many small ways that individuals strive for a more common purpose.

You can look for existing opportunities to join in with cross-department or whole-school projects or, failing that, see if you can start one yourself. Examples include:

- Duke of Edinburgh Award
- The British Council 'International School' award
- Arts Mark
- Eco Schools
- Stonewall 'Awards for School Champions'

It has also been suggested that being part of a mentoring/coaching relationship can help schools which are experiencing balkanisation (Beatty, 2000). In an ideal world, this would be a whole-school approach. However, developing a mentor relationship by yourself is similar to having a critical friend, although it can be a more formal relationship. The benefit to a teacher experiencing balkanisation is that they can look outside of their group and gain a different perspective.

Finding a mentor is daunting and needs preparation. There are several key questions to ask yourself about whom you wish to approach:

1. Have they shown any previous interest in your career?
2. Do they have an existing professional experience of you such as through attending courses with each other?
3. Do they have the knowledge and experience you feel you would benefit from?

4. Is there anything they have achieved in your school that you admire or respect?
5. Do you think they have the time to meet with you on a regular basis?

Brendan experienced balkanisation in two different schools and used mentoring as a way to cope. In the first of these he was finding it challenging having a class with complex profound and multiple learning difficulties (PMLD). There was a more experienced LSA who worked in another PMLD class and Brendan had been awed by how she had led an inclusive and meaningful class assembly. He approached her and explained that he'd had little first-hand experience with such a group and would love to get some tips and advice. This informal conversation led to regular meetings where he felt that he could get answers to questions no one had taught him at university. In his second experience of a balkanised school, he used the same technique again, this time approaching a senior leader who had come from a mainstream setting because he wanted to develop a more rounded understanding of teaching, learning and assessment outside of a special school environment.

Neither of these mentoring relationships was formal and they were not part of the whole-school culture. Instead they were informally arranged and ended up making him feel less isolated within the groups he had ended up in.

Individualism

Individualist schools are very isolating to work in and can stifle personal development as you tend to teach in the same way year after year even when you know that some parts of your practice are not as strong as they could be. There are two types of settings: environmental and psychological. Environmentally structured individualist schools are sometimes called 'egg crate' settings as they are built around keeping individual classrooms and staff separate from each other. Psychological individualism is where we staff feel isolated due to our state of mind. Neither is more important than the other but the potential remedies are the same.

Surviving in a school like this is about taking the initiative to develop yourself. There are two ways to do this: develop collaboration in your school and find ways to collaborate outside of your school. In-school collaboration is similar to developing a critical friend, except that instead of looking at your wider life, the focus is specifically on your practice and is a two-way experience. It is a chance to share ideas, joint plan, or develop a new resource. You may find that such low-level collaboration is hard to set up if individualism is deeply entrenched in the school or if there is a fear of sharing practice. That's when looking to collaborate outside of school is beneficial (although it is important to note that external collaboration is beneficial in its own right) as there are numerous ways you can develop support networks.

Support networks take many forms including face-to-face meet-ups, and social media. Face-to-face activities include joining teaching organisations who run conferences or regional events. Many events happen on a Saturday, are reasonably priced, and may offer childcare. The benefit of this for teachers in schools experiencing a culture of individualism is that there is no need to request time off work to attend, which many may feel uncomfortable doing. There are general groups which cover the whole of the profession and those specifically for specialist areas such as SEN or research.

The growth in social media over the past decade has created a range of opportunities for teachers. Twitter has become a focus for teachers networking, sharing resources and having a space to ask professional questions. It is also a great place to keep in touch with educational research and new initiatives. The benefit for teachers is that you can become as engaged as you want to and you have the freedom to dip in and out of what is going on and choose who you wish to follow.

Both Richard and Brendan are avid users of Twitter, although they take different approaches. Richard often follows conversations or chats, making comments when he wants to, but largely observes from a distance. His profile is very basic and although he follows a lot of educational professionals, he doesn't engage with them on a regular basis. Brendan is the polar opposite. He is an active member of many Twitter groups, regularly tweets and responds to comments from others, and shares research and resources. Neither approach is wrong; they are simply two examples of teachers who began using social media to collaborate with others when their schools did not offer them such opportunities.

Groupthink

Surviving in a groupthink school can be tough as it means you are constantly swimming against the tide if you are choosing not to join in. It can be even more challenging if, like several of our teachers, you are the victim of such a mindset. This can lead to isolation from colleagues, anxiety about going to work, and a constant fear that maybe you are wrong and everyone else is right. It feels like you only have a few choices depending upon the specific circumstances:

1. Leave.
2. Take a stand.
3. Join in.

Leaving isn't an immediate option for everyone, and unless you already have a plan for what you are going to do, it can have emotional and financial implications. Taking a stand isn't straightforward either, especially if you are a lone voice arguing against a whole-school culture. In this case, you run the risk of further alienation and, in the worst case, a deliberate attempt to engineer you to a point where you wish to leave. That leaves joining in, which many teachers eventually do even if they are only giving lip service to the SLT. The danger of this path is that somewhere along the way, you begin to agree with the culture you were so previously adamantly against and lose sight of your own philosophy and values. Sounds bleak. But there is a fourth way: acceptance.

This stance is about accepting the way that your current school works, trying to understand why that groupthink mentality is present, and self-reflection so that you are able to maintain your own values. Acceptance is not the same as being complicit. Acceptance doesn't mean that you agree with the groupthink or want any part in it. Instead it is about freeing yourself from the pressures of thinking that you could, or should, change it. It is also about trying to remove yourself from the situation and not see the groupthink mentality as a personal attack on you. If we can rationalise our thoughts and see groupthink as a specific type of social behaviour, then we are on the way to limiting the emotional impact on ourselves.

This limitation of emotional impact is why it is important to understand how that groupthink came to be. The seeds were sown before your arrival in the school and before any course of action you might have taken. There are many reasons why a groupthink mentality might exist. For some groups, it is to do with a crisis and much research has been conducted to evaluate the effect a high-stress event can have on a group; it makes the group mentality stronger, such as seen in the close-knit relationships in the armed forces during conflict (Janis, 1972). For others, the groupthink arises due to a natural tendency for humans to seek to be around those that think and feel as they do as it gives a sense of security by sharing in a familiar set of group behaviours (Hogg and Reid, 2006). In both cases, the groupthink mentality offers a place for staff to feel safe and secure. Understanding why the groupthink mentality exists can help you to decide how you will respond.

Choosing how to act is about understanding who you are, what values you hold, and where you wish your teaching journey to go. For Richard, the groupthink mentality came out of a crisis of his own making: his affair. He knew that he was not going to be able to change the mindset of those he was working with; but neither was he in a position to resign as he had nothing lined up to go to. Instead he had to accept the position he was in – including his own part in it – and try to gain some mental distance from the situation until he was able to leave. If you do decide that the groupthink mentally has overspilled into workplace bullying, you need to gather evidence and ultimately contact your union for support.

Bibliography

Beatty, B. R. (2000) 'Teachers leading their own professional growth: self-directed reflection and collaboration and changes in perception of self and work in secondary school teachers', *Journal of In-Service Education* 26 (1) pp. 73–97.

Hargreaves, A. (2001) 'Emotional geographies of teaching', *Teachers College Record* 103 (6) pp. 1056–1080.

Hogg, M. A. and Reid, S. A. (2006) 'Social identity, self-categorization, and the communication of group norms', *Communication Theory* 16 (1) pp. 7–30.

Janis, I. L. (1972) *Victims of groupthink: a psychological study of foreign-policy decisions and fiascoes*. Oxford: Houghton Mifflin.

Reflections

Chapter 10 – Coping as a leader in a toxic school: the eight characteristics

In the previous chapter, we looked at how to cope in a toxic school as a teacher. Here we focus more on leadership roles with a specific focus on what leaders can do to change these eight characteristics if they encounter toxicity in the setting they work in.

High staff turnover

People leave posts for all sorts of reasons; sometimes people leave simply because the school isn't right for them. This need not be because the school is toxic: you might be a leader in a school in a challenging area which some of your staff were not fully prepared for; or you might have had several staff looking for promotions which you could not offer. The important thing is knowing *why* people are leaving and assessing if there is anything about the culture of your school that is helping them to make that choice.

When we are in the midst of school life, it is hard to make value judgements about our setting, especially when you may be on the treadmill of gathering evidence for a future Ofsted or have had to re-home all of Key Stage 1 due to asbestos in the building. It takes a degree of bravery to take a step back and look objectively at your setting when you are so deeply involved in a relationship with it. There are two issues to being reflective about your school: culture and systems.

We hear a lot about 'culture' – to the degree that it may make us stop listening. Don't. The culture of a school is vital in retaining and attracting staff and covers everything from the gut feeling you get when you walk in to the relationships between staff. We have all probably been to schools, walked into the main office, and made a snap judgement about what the culture is like simply by talking to the reception staff. It is with these fresh eyes that you need to view your own setting and be prepared to drop your guard and assumptions – leave them at the door. Spending half an hour walking around the site with this attitude can tell you a lot. Do you hear raised voices from staff? Are people in the staffroom chatting at break times? Are the reception staff greeting visitors and pupils with a smile? Do the corridors and classrooms feel welcoming?

One way of doing an assessment like this is to look at the school from the perspective of one of your staff. Pick a name at random or use a name of someone who has applied for other posts – or has been successful in obtaining one. Plan several questions to ask as you walk around. These could be:

- Does the member of staff have easy access to facilities such as a toilet and staffroom?
- Who do they seem to socialise with? Are they positive or negative influences?
- How would they perceive the latest policy change/new intervention/CPD and its impact upon their classroom?
- When was the last time you spoke to them? What was it about?
- Have they ever approached you for support?
- What about their daily experience in the school? What would they rate as a positive and what as a negative? Why?
- Do you know if they have a family?

In order to reduce staff turnover, we as leaders need to make the whole staff team feel welcomed and valued in our schools by ensuring they have a positive experience at work (Fullan, 2002). This need not be a huge task to undertake even if you have a large staff team as there are simple ideas you could use. One school I worked in had a headteacher who recorded staff birthdays in her diary when she employed them. Each year a birthday card would arrive in your pigeonhole. This was a beautifully simple act and she did this for all staff in the setting, which was close to 80 people. Other ways could include making sure that the staffroom is properly equipped, that staff have some flexibility for childcare or care of elderly parents, that you know the name of everyone in the school and find time to say hello and have a general chat when you can.

Schools are staffed by humans with all of the emotions and experiences they bring. Working with young people can be incredibly rewarding, yet also highly draining. By building a culture around drawing out and developing positive human relationships, we can make schools more rewarding places to work in.

A 'sinking' school

If you are a leader in a sinking school, your daily issues are almost the exact opposite of the type of school discussed above. Instead of a high turnover of staff and a lack of continuity, you are faced with a staff team which is slowly stagnating and hesitant to any form of change. This is especially tough if you have joined the school as a new leader. Winning around a staff team like this is tough and successes are not going to happen overnight.

Coping as a leader in a sinking school is about planning and persistence and going through a process of 're-culturing' the school by transforming staff, pupil, and community mindsets (Stoll, 1998). Staff in such settings are tough audiences, and bringing in any new initiatives may make you feel like a stand-up comedian bombing a routine on stage: you may get limited feedback and things you are excited about may fall flat. Plus, pushing too much change in a short time could lose any staff support for the future. So you need to plan carefully. Take time to look at the school's improvement plan and prioritise what developments you need to make. The pressure might be on to improve the quality of writing; however, you may want to pick something else to start with to get a short-term win. Give staff plenty of notice about meetings, CPD, learning walks etc. Having a clear calendar and friendly reminders can help prepare staff for change.

Planning your time over a full school year means you can build in occasions to recap key elements and keep the momentum going; often it is the lack of drive and enthusiasm from staff that leads new initiatives to fall flat. You also need to pace yourself. You will largely be driving this yourself until you have developed relationships to the degree that you have found some allies. Pacing yourself is important and a good mantra to have is 'hasten slowly'. This is a balance between acting and reflecting, and reflection is crucial. This is where persistence comes into to play. If you persist at pushing a new initiative in a certain way again and again, you will lose people. Instead, through reflection, you are going to need to adapt your approach to suit the situation. Say you have introduced a new planning template in a staff meeting in September and it is still not being used by all staff at the end of term. Having another staff meeting to go over it again will probably not engage the staff that you hadn't previously and will only alienate the staff you already had on your side. You need to do something different. This may be as simple as having an outside visitor from another school explain how they plan, using a book club approach to look at good practice in a recent education publication, or arranging for staff to meet in cross-department or Key Stage solution circles to problem-solve how the planning template is being used and where staff feel it could be improved.

A 'hothouse' school

One of the dangers of leadership is simply not realising when you need to take your foot off the pedal and give your staff time to breathe. It is all about reflection: why are you piling the pressure on to staff in the first place? Is the pressure having the desired effect? If you are new to leadership or new to a post, you may have a natural desire to want to impress or make quick changes; but the result for staff can be that too much changes too soon with little time to adjust and no sense of collaboration. If you are in a school which is preparing for the next inspection, then the pressure may be coming from the top down, as Richard experienced in chapter 4. Either way, there can often be a disconnect between what leaders expect staff to do and what they would have previously been happy to be asked to do.

Part of being a leader in a hothouse school is evaluating the necessity of all the added pressure and making adjustments to it where required. This is where there is a distinct benefit in engaging with academic research so that you make every training session or new initiative relative. For example, if your SLT expects staff to plan for different learning styles, or it wants to see brain gym starter activities on a learning walk, then you really need to investigate what is actually effective and what is just a fad.

> Educational fads! We've all been there. The worst ones seem to come and go each year. In a toxic school, this is often driven by compliance rather than capability, and by the leadership or context of the school. Ask any teacher and they'll be able to recount the initiatives and new policies introduced at the start of each academic year. They're tiresome, unnecessary and generally don't motivate teachers. Worse? They are quite often lacking any substance or backed by any academic research to help improve classroom performance. Rather than explain each one, I've left you with a list of teaching fad headings to wince over. If you can nod your head to over half of these, then you may need to look up and ask yourself: 'Do I work in a toxic school?' If you do, find the nearest exit!
>
> 1. Marking by frequency
> 2. The purple pen of progress
> 3. Verbal feedback stamps or tracking dialogic marking
> 4. Behaviour policies and systems that the teachers finds too hard to understand
> 5. Three-part lessons – five or seven parts too!

6. Detailed lesson plans
7. Collecting evidence for performance management targets you didn't set
8. Recording lesson objectives every lesson
9. Fine grading A–G grades, e.g. A1, A2, A3 ... or 9.1, 9.2, 9.3
10. Lolly-stick questioning
11. Learning styles on lesson plans
12. Triple marking
13. Shanghai maths
14. Starters, middles and plenaries in every lesson
15. Performing to the observer's tickbox during observation
16. Brain gym
17. Zero tolerance
18. Ten-page department self-evaluations that mimic school evaluation
19. Training days where nobody has a say

I'll stop there! Any missing?

Engaging with research is not something you should fear and there are some easy ways that you can add it into your work life without it taking over – and without having to study for a further qualification (unless you want to). Social media is a great way of getting recommendations about how research can be used within your school and there are group chats specifically about research that you can join. You can also join teaching organisations that offer you access to their own journals or use Google Scholar to find open-access PDFs that you can read for free. The most important thing is not to be scared by it but engage with it and see how relevant it can be for deciding the focus for staff training or long-term improvement planning.

An important thing to remember is that no one is suggesting that schools should be without any pressure or expectations placed upon staff. Pressure does not always have to be negative and 'positive pressure' can be highly motivating for staff to achieve sustainable change with measurable outcomes (Fullan, 2010).

Repeated restructuring

Restructuring is a tough experience for everyone to go though but many forget the toll it takes on leaders. You may be making decisions about changing your whole setting due to cuts in finances or a difficult inspection, and decisions about roles and pay scales can be tough, especially when you know that it is affecting the real lives of the staff in your setting. What makes restructuring toxic is when it is either repeated time and time again, putting staff through the stress and anxiety of the whole process, or it is not transparent so that everyone knows what is happening and why.

To prevent this, it is important to try to get it right first time and answer a fundamental question: 'Why are we here?' Understanding the purpose of your school can help to clarify what your school vision could become, and it is this clear articulation of a purpose which your culture is built upon. This all stems from having a vision for your school which has not only been thoroughly researched but also shared with staff. If staff know where the school is going, and feel part of the process, they will find future changes easier to manage. As the leaders, you are accountable for how this vision is shared and for making the process as clear as possible. Decisions which are made entirely behind closed doors and are not expressed to those they involve show a lack of trust and regard for the staff team. Whilst such openness may not always be possible, especially if there are cuts to posts, engaging staff with the process as much as you can is ideal.

Bureaucratic

As we discussed in chapter 9, bureaucratic schools can be effective and positive places to work, especially for emerging leaders, who can often find opportunities to develop in a supportive and clear system (Parlar and Ramazan, 2017). The problem with being a leader in a bureaucratic school is that it might work for you, but does it work for those you lead? If your setting is one where the bureaucracy is stifling staff, then you need to be prepared to make some adaptations. You may not be in a position to change the whole school ethos but you can make changes within your department or area of responsibility. These changes are not big but can have a huge impact. They are:

1. Authenticity
2. Collaboration
3. Investment

Being an authentic leader is about having a genuine relationship with those you lead. It has a moral and ethical basis as it is about making decisions and choices as yourself rather than becoming a stereotype of what you *think* a leader should be; it is about self-awareness of how you act, think, and behave; it is an awareness of how you are perceived by other people in your setting – and especially by those you lead (Avolio and Gardner, 2005). We can sum it up as having integrity and approaching leadership as part of a relationship with staff rather than as a role to perform.

There is a great deal of research into what authenticity in leadership actually looks like; however, Avolio and Gardner's succinct list is a good starting place. They identify the following key features:

- Positive psychological outlook – being optimistic, hopeful, resilient and confident in your approach to leadership and decision making
- Positive moral purpose – an ethical and moral outlook to leadership which affects the decisions you make or how you express to others
- Self-awareness – not only of who you are as a person but how you act
- Self-regulation – making sure that your actions remain in line with your moral compass
- Leadership behaviours – how you influence other people and how you model the behaviours you expect others to demonstrate

- Follower self-awareness/regulation – the impact you as a leader have on developing these characteristics in your team
- Follower development – due to an ongoing open and honest relationship between yourself and your team there should develop and ongoing cycle of you developing the skills if those you lead and, in turn, your own skills developing

Collaborative working is important in a bureaucratic school because it allows staff to feel involved in developing the ethos and culture of the setting. The danger in bureaucratic schools is that decisions are imposed upon staff from above and enforced by leaders at different levels. This gives staff little scope to voice their own contributions and influence the school's culture. As a leader, you may also miss out on ideas and suggestions from unlikely sources: you will have a wealth of information and knowledge in your setting if you would only take the time to listen to it.

Collaborative working and a focus on collaborative leadership can also enable cultural changes to be implemented and sustained to their fruition, as well as creating greater cohesion between staff (Copland, 2003). Yet it is not just staff who benefit: a collaborative approach to leadership can also improve the attainment of pupils (Hallinger and Heck, 2011).

The final change that can be made is investing in staff. Whilst this may have a financial element in terms of allowing – and encouraging – staff to attend paid CPD, there are also many ways that you can invest in staff with little or no financial implications. Whether or not there is a cost, investing in staff boosts more than just the staff member involved: it allows for innovation which can support schools in weathering the wider educational culture (Collinson et al., 2009). It is important for leaders to remember that it can also have an impact on pupil progress if training is carefully chosen (Flecknoe, 2000).

Whilst some CPD has financial implications, such as National Professional Qualification for Middle Leadership (NPQML) courses, investing in staff is also about *time*. This can be as simple as ensuring that staff have adequate time during the week to not only plan and prepare but also engage with research or collocation with colleagues in school and in other settings. Research by the OECD compared face-to-face teaching hours across the year in a variety of different countries. As an example, a Key Stage 3 teacher in the UK spends roughly 65% of their time teaching and has over 800 contact hours a year (OECD, 2017).

Finding creative ways to reduce this contact time over a week can give staff some additional time for their own personal development. How each school approaches this depends upon their specific circumstances, but ideas often used include an assembly rota so that not all staff are present on every occasion, using timetabling software to make best use of every minute, and extending the school day to include afternoon activities staffed by specialists. At a department level you could turn every other departmental meeting into a research session or encourage staff to access social media sites such as Twitter, where they can access their own CPD for free through the connections they make.

Balkanisation

Leadership in a balkanised school can be tough as there are differing mindsets and often a lack of uniformity in approach and opinion. Getting a staff team behind you is a challenge because there is always the risk that you will be seen to be alienating one group in favour of meeting another's needs.

The important thing as a leader is to understand why the balkanisation happened as this will effect how you approach dealing with it. There are two main routes to balkanisation:

1. Structural balkanisation – often found in large schools, especially secondary, through a rigid departmental structure
2. Event balkanisation – often occurs when there is a dramatic cultural change, such as a new school leader, restructuring, or suspensions within the staff team

Structural balkanisation often manifests itself in schools which have clear departments in set areas of a school. For example, staff teaching science may largely spend time with other science staff, including sharing break and lunch times with them. They may not regularly meet with other staff except in whole-school meetings. In such meetings, staff teams will often sit with each other and attempts to mix staff up between departments can be met with some hostility. Departments will develop their own narratives about others departments in school, so the English department may be perceived to be 'set in their ways' or EYFS might be seen as 'insular'. The narratives will vary from school to school depending upon the history and context of the setting. Understanding these narratives is crucial for breaking down structural balkanisation.

Hearing these narratives takes time and some detective work, especially when you are an outsider to any of the groups. You may well know how your own Key Stage or department views others as you are within the fold, but it is somewhat harder to know how others view your own group. It is important that you develop a wide range of relationships across all of the groups in your setting. If staff see that you are genuinely interested in their needs, views, and vision, then some will open up to you. Once you know where each group places itself in relation to the others, you can start to break down some of those barriers. You may encounter some hostility to start with, but you have to persist. Breaking these barriers is less about forced cross-group work in staff meetings and more about creating opportunities for staff to mix on a regular basis. Cross-department work to apply for funding, achieve a school award, or run a community event gives space for staff to mix in a voluntary capacity and allows relationships to develop naturally.

Event balkanisation is a harder divide to heal. Jessica was in a leadership position during her head's suspension and a divide appeared between those who remained loyal to the head and those who had felt that the leadership of the school was lacking. Brendan experienced event balkanisation when his school experienced a challenging Ofsted which ended the supportive and collaborative environment he was used to working in. In both cases, those teachers left the schools they were in as leadership was unable to heal the wounds. So, what could the leaders in both schools have done?

Firstly, there is a need for leaders to acknowledge that there are issues in the first place. You may be so caught up in the event itself that you fail to recognise the impact it is having on the wider staff team. This can be prevented by having a degree of transparency about what is happening and making it a priority to support staff with their own experiences. Staff who see an SLT shut away will naturally begin to feel anxious and unsettled, which can lead to deep divides across all staff groups as rumours and gossip spread. Humans respond in different ways to traumatic events and an understanding of this is crucial. Research into Post-traumatic stress disorder (PTSD) in adults (Breslau, 2012) has shown four elements that affect an adult's ability to cope with trauma:

1. Personality
2. Pre-existing mental health issues
3. Amount of social support available
4. The ability to reason, rationalise, and plan

This means that, as a leader, you need to provide different types of support. Some staff may need access to counselling; some may want to seek advice from their union; some may just prefer to keep their head down and get on with it. Support may also need to be ongoing for several months or, in some cases, years. Leaders shouldn't judge staff in a negative light if they are not 'cured' in the timescale which SLT have decided. For some, the event at work might have awoken other concerns in their personal lives. For others, it might be months or years down the line that another event awakens the trauma from work. From my own experience, it was not until a very close relative was suddenly taken seriously ill that events in my personal and professional life from many years ago raised their head and I had a crisis moment out of the blue. We are all different and there is no single right way to deal with trauma.

Secondly, preventing event balkanisation from happening at all is crucial as it is difficult to rejoin the groups once they have separated. This can be achieved through whole-school information sharing so that one group is not partial to more information than any other. Resentment can easily set in if the Key Stage 1 lead who is also the deputy head tells his team about what is happening behind the SLT closed door when Key Stage 2 are left in the dark. The key is planning for a crisis before it happens by having a leadership that is aware of crisis-management strategies. No organisation can totally avoid experiencing crisis moments, and therefore a crisis-management plan is a positive way of preparing for an event and knowing how you are going to cope in the aftermath (Coombs, 2014). A plan could be stored in a file (both electronic and printed stored securely) which includes the following:

- Contact details of those in the local authority that the SLT can call for support (as well as their roles and responsibilities), including the local authority media and legal teams
- Details of how information will be disseminated to staff
- A staff policy for dealing with the media and external complaints
- A staff policy for supporting mental health and wellbeing
- Contact details for support services, including counselling, educational psychology, and unions

Leading in a balkanised school is challenging and there are no quick fixes. It takes resilience and it is beneficial to have your own support strategies in place.

Individualism

Being a leader in a school with a strong individualist perspective means you are often out looking for staff as they may well spend a lot of their non-contact time within their own classrooms instead of mixing in the staffroom or other communal areas. Any attempt to force collaborative working as a whole-school approach will be met with resentment and a sense of fear. As a leader, jumping in with your big boots and organising something on a large scale will probably backfire and you may end up alienating yourself.

Changing this mindset is about a long-term cultural change. This is not going to happen overnight or with one staff meeting; instead, it requires investment of time, CPD, and ongoing engagement with staff throughout the process. It is also important for the headteacher to be a visible promoter of change (Waldron and McLeskey, 2010). Research has shown that it is challenging for NQTs to begin their careers in a culture of individualism (Williams et al., 2001) so it is not too much of a leap to consider the implications of one for early-career staff or those who join the setting. Richard and Brendan both experienced the challenge of joining a school where individualism was part of the accepted practice, and Richard's attempts to create a more collaborative setting went unsupported by the SLT and were viewed as a negative act. This shows the importance of leadership being behind such a change.

But what can you do if you do not have the support of your headteacher? Your chance of changing the whole culture is certainly hugely decreased, but this does not mean that you cannot have some impact with some groups. It may be that this influence is enough to start a slow spread of ideas, although they may not be sustainable in the long term and may always remain low key. Firstly, if possible try to understand why the culture of individualism has developed in the first place. If you know what the trigger was, you will be better placed to know how to go about changing it. Secondly, find where there are already some collaborative elements of practice, such as in classes that have a teacher and LSA or that have job-share staff. Are there any hints and tips that these staff are able to share with others? For example, do they make use of online cloud storage to share planning or use a group chat to feed back about any key events that have happened? Finally, organise CPD which has collaboration built in rather than being about collaboration per se. The moment some staff get wind that they will be learning how to work with each other, you will lose them. Yet if the CPD is on a topic which is entirely different but contains some elements of collaborative practice to build staff understanding of it, they may be none the wiser.

Groupthink

How you lead in a setting which has a groupthink mentality depends upon whether you are within the group or are the individual who remains on the outside. If you are the outsider in a leadership role, as Jessica was, you have to act very carefully. You have similar options to a teacher in the same situation: you can choose to leave or take a stand. Jessica initially took a stand against the SLT members that she felt were encouraging other staff to rebel against decisions she was making. When the previous deputy head died of cancer just before Christmas, Jessica felt that the only option was to leave; the grief experienced by staff seemed to intensify the groupthink attitude towards her.

If Jessica had decided to stay, what could she have done? Jessica did make use of some of her allies within the setting but these people were powerless to support her at the level she needed. One avenue is to meticulously log and record every incident which you experience, as the groupthink could overspill into direct bullying – which is what Brendan experienced as a teacher. There are added concerns if you are in a leadership position because you may be having your role undermined by others. Make sure that all of the leadership tasks you do, suggestions you make, or new strategies you bring in are recorded in email. This includes copying other SLT members into emails asking staff to complete tasks you have set them. Then, if you need it, you have a body of evidence behind you – particularly useful if you are concerned that you may face a challenging performance-management meeting.

This evidence is also useful if you choose to leave. You may be worried about getting a not-too-glowing reference from your head so it's a good idea to create your own evidence file of all the work you have done. This is something that you can take with you to interviews and use as a point of discussion. It can include anonymised emails as well as physical copies of resources you have made. If your head does not mention any of your good practice, then you at least have evidence that it happened and that staff at all levels were involved.

Bibliography

Avolio, B. J. and Gardner, W. L. (2005) 'Authentic leadership development: getting to the root of positive forms of leadership', *The Leadership Quarterly* 16 (3) pp. 315–338.

Breslau, N. (2012) 'Epidemiology of posttraumatic stress disorder in adults' in Beck, J. G. and Sloan, D. M. (eds) *The Oxford handbook of traumatic stress disorders*. New York, NY: Oxford University Press, pp. 84–97.

Collinson, V., Kozina, E., Lin, Y.-H. K., Ling, L., Matheson, I., Newcombe, L. and Zogla, I. (2009) 'Professional development for teachers: a world of change', *European Journal of Teacher Education* 32 (1) pp. 3–19.

Coombs, W. T. (2014) *Ongoing crisis communication: planning, managing, and responding.* Thousand Oaks, CA: SAGE Publications.

Copland, M. A. (2003) 'Leadership of inquiry: building and sustaining capacity for school improvement', *Educational Evaluation and Policy Analysis* 25 (4) pp. 375–395.

Flecknoe, M. (2000) 'Can continuing professional development for teachers be shown to raise pupils' achievement?', *Journal of In-Service Education* 26 (3) pp. 437–457.

Fullan, M. (2002) 'Principals as leaders in a culture of change', *Educational Leadership* 59 (8) pp. 16–21.

Fullan, M. (2010) 'Positive Pressure' in Hargreaves, A., Liberman, A., Fullan, M. and Hopkins, D. (eds) *Second international handbook of educational change.* Dordrecht: Springer Science+Business Media, pp. 119–130.

Hallinger, P. and Heck, R. H. (2011) 'Collaborative leadership and school improvement: understanding the impact on school capacity and student learning' in Townsend, T. and MacBeath, J. (eds) *International handbook of leadership for learning.* Dordrecht: Springer, pp. 469–485.

OECD (2017) *Education at a glance 2017: OECD indicators.* Paris: OECD Publishing.

Parlar, H. and Ramazan, C. (2017) 'The effect of bureaucratic school structure on teacher leadership culture: a mixed study', *Educational Sciences: Theory and Practice* 17 (6) pp. 2175–2201.

Stoll, L. (1998) 'School culture', *School Improvement Network's Bulletin* 9.

Waldron, N. L. and McLeskey, J. (2010) 'Establishing a collaborative school culture through comprehensive school reform', *Journal of Educational and Psychological Consultation* 20 (1) pp. 58–74.

Williams, A., Prestage, S. and Bedward, J. (2001) 'Individualism to collaboration: the significance of teacher culture to the induction of newly qualified teachers', *Journal of Education for Teaching* 27 (3) pp. 253–267.

Reflections

Chapter 11 – Teacher voice, identity, and ethnographic research: a way forward?

To become free, teachers must govern themselves; but how we do this is another matter. One way we can start to see this happening is in the grassroots vision set out by the Chartered College of Teaching in England. The College is a new professional body for students, teachers, and colleagues working alongside teachers. One of their main aims is to bridge the gap between research and the reality of classrooms to provide a safe community where teachers can share practice, ideas, and support. Longer term, the College intends to sustain the English Teachers' Standards and begin to inform government policy.

Why is it important? Well, wellbeing and teacher-voice research suggests that teachers want three things to achieve greater success – beyond the realms of examinations and league tables. As highlighted in *Flip The System* (2015) by Jelmer Evers and René Kneyber:

1. Teachers spend a long time developing skills and should enjoy their work. They should foster a curiosity for improving their practice and follow this through in collaboration with others.

2. Teachers should have a sense of professional pride in their achievements and will seek ways to gain the acknowledgement from others. However, the outside world – which is market orientated – might have a different set of standards from those of the teacher. Professional pride should therefore always strive to reach middle ground between humility and cockiness.
3. Professional honour and recognition has to be earned. Teachers must expect high standards of themselves and each other in order to be trusted by the rest of society.

As highlighted in the research by Professor Becky Allen and Dr Sam Sims (*The Teacher Gap*, 2018), 'Teachers rely ... on a subtle process of pattern recognition, in which they draw analogies with their internal database of similar past experiences.'

It's very clear to me from my 17 years of leadership experience: if you want to bring teachers along with you, teacher voice matters.

Teacher voice

Why is teacher voice important? Firstly, teachers who are able to express their own voices with competence are able to support pupils in having their voices heard. Research into how teachers felt about pupil voice in the classroom highlighted that it is often the pupils who don't express their voices that are the ones that most need to be heard (McIntyre et al., 2005). This naturally requires some dedication from teachers to actively hear what these pupils have to say. However, this mutual relationship of hearing and trusting can develop both the pupil's and the teacher's ability to share their voice – and is therefore beneficial to teachers. Lincoln (1995, p. 93) sums it up like this:

> Teachers can elicit student voices. And teachers can, in the process, be led to discover their own voices. One cannot happen without the other, but happily the achievement of voice is mutual, and teachers who help students to find student voices will discover that their own voices are clearer and stronger in the process.

Secondly, the stories that teachers tell are important; there is a wealth of knowledge from inside the classroom that needs to be 'voiced' (Elbaz, 1991) so that others can benefit. Hearing these voices can improve classroom relationships, reduce teacher turnover and improve academic outcomes too. This might sound too idealistic but stop and reflect for a moment. How different could the experiences of our five teachers have been if they had experienced an educational culture where the lived experiences of other teachers had been accessible at the crisis moments in their careers? What could they have learnt from others about how to cope or where to turn for support? If we dare to think bigger and look at the wider school culture, then the impact of teacher voice can have an even more dramatic effect. If our school leaders are mindful of their schools becoming toxic – and act decisively to ensure that issues are quickly addressed if they do – we could see a reduction in effect on teachers as a whole. As we discussed in chapter 2, a happier workforce creates a better classroom climate and impacts upon pupil outcomes. This might be idealistic but surely we need to have the vision in mind to work towards?

Thirdly, teacher voice is closely tied to teacher identity; the experience of lacking a voice can change the way that teachers view their role and can limit their own personal development. Goodson's understanding of teacher voice goes beyond that which relates solely to their professional practice, instead locating the importance of having their voices heard as part of their wider lives (Goodson, 1991). He suggests several reasons for this, including the impact of our life experiences on who we are. We are more than just an adult in a classroom who becomes a 'teacher' the moment we cross the threshold of our school. We bring into our classrooms our childhood, our own educational experiences, our family lives, our relationships, our successes, and our failures. We bring our entire identity with us. This was something I realised I did with my own class; my relationships with them were at their deepest when I was being fully myself. We will discuss identity further in the following section.

Finally, sharing our voice – freedom of expression – is a human right found in Article 10 of the Human Rights Act from 1998. It is a fundamental human entitlement and therefore we should protect and facilitate it rather than shy away from it.

The concept of teacher voice is not a singular one. It has been acknowledged that it is woven from several different threads which could be loosely called authenticity, the right to speak and the right to have a political voice (Brindley, 2015). However, I would argue that an authentic teacher voice encompasses all other expressions within a complex and messy system, just as we see with the concept of authentic pupil voice. One of my resounding feelings from teaching is the frustration that my professional voice has often been silenced as the voices of teachers are often undervalued. When this is compared to the growing importance of pupil voice, teacher voice stands in stark contrast as being gradually undermined rather than developed and celebrated (Bragg, 2007; Brindley, 2015). This undermining has affected teachers at national, local and classroom levels.

Nationally, the introduction of the national curriculum and a centralised approach to teaching was seen by many as containing a hidden agenda to limit the voices of teachers who were mistrusted in political circles (Barber and Graham, 2013). The role of teachers in being in control of their classroom and having professional freedom had ended and a new era of control and conformity arose. It was within this system that I trained to be a teacher, that I learnt how to implement the required methods and plan for the given units. The fact that I once taught a unit about the seaside to a class who had never seen the sea did not matter – that was what the curriculum said and that is what you must do. Anyway, whom would I have discussed it with? Who would have heard my voice? Any concerns I had were silenced by the enforcement of education policy.

You do not have to look too far on Twitter today to see a mistrust of those teachers who are deemed to be part of government policy-making by those who feel that the decisions made are at odds with their own education philosophy. Some recent changes in education policy and direction have been widely dismissed by teachers, yet even in this case it is the voice of the unions that is most clearly heard as representatives of teachers' voices. Teachers are the objects of educational policy-making and not active, voiced participants (Hargreaves and Shirley, 2012). The lived experiences of teachers and their opinions have diminished to the pages of blogs where teachers pour out their thoughts and feelings from behind the veil of anonymity, such as *The Secret Teacher from The Guardian*. This is not what authentic teacher voice should look like. It also shows that teachers are not skilled at knowing how to share their voice (Stitzlein and Quinn, 2012), which leads to the question of how this can be better supported. The growth of social media use by teachers has opened a void in adequately supporting teachers to use these tools in an ethical and professional way. Instead those of us who have turned to social media to have our voices heard have largely learnt by the mistakes we have made and from guidance from more experienced users.

There is also a great fear of using social media to express voice. If you look at the Twitter bios of many teachers, they contain a caveat of 'all views my own' or similar. Teachers across all social media platforms feel a need to protect their professional life and specific job so that nothing they say or imply can be used against them in case of a legal dispute or work against them (Papandrea, 2012; Goodson and Numan, 2002). This feeling of fear is widespread throughout many organisations; making one's voice heard could potentially be seen as going against the system, turning concerned employees into potential whistleblowers (Burke and Cooper, 2013). The government definition says that 'you're a whistleblower if you're a worker and you report certain types of wrongdoing'. Does the average teacher in a school setting know where the grey line is drawn between raising a comment in an online Twitter debate and potentially discussing something which an employer could deem to be whistleblowing?

The Secret Teacher: Dispatches from the Classroom (Anon, 2017), a popular book published in 2017, details the teaching experiences of an anonymous secondary school teacher. This honest and vivid account, depicting a working life that so many of us can resonate with – both the highs and the lows – could never have been written with the author's name disclosed. This is entirely understandable in this specific situation: I am sure many teachers would also want to remain anonymous if they were talking about their professional experiences. Reading such an open account should make our own self-censoring of our views on Ofsted, new government policy, or the publicly shared practice of another school, diminish in size. But still we hide.

There have been positive changes in education. Over the past few years, for example, there has been an increase in grassroots teaching communities. These vary from general teaching networks, such as the Chartered College of Teaching, to those with a specific focus, such as WomenEd. There is a long history of grassroots movements in global education reform (Reese, 2002); however, the growth of social media discussed above has led to a far larger audience than ever before. Nevertheless, I would argue that the impact of teachers being able to have a nationally heard voice is limited unless their voices are heard at a local and individual school level. A teacher who is aware of wider practices in education yet remains unheard within their own setting will become increasingly frustrated and isolated.

The hierarchical nature of educational establishments often means that there is little scope for teachers to have their voices heard; those higher up take precedence (Alamri, 2015). Whilst this is professionally sound in the majority of cases, surely limiting a teacher's capacity to raise concerns over policy or to question an accepted practice hampers the development of the profession? Increasing conformity to practices which run counter to deeply held professional values limits the necessary debate and discussion which is crucial in allowing teaching to develop.

The hierarchical nature of educational establishments also leads to problems for teachers having their voices heard at a classroom level. Here, teachers can find their voices silenced by leadership (Dana, 1995), leaving them with similar feelings of disenfranchisement within their own classrooms. Yet this need not be the case: leaders who listen to the voices of their teachers raise a teacher's self esteem and motivation (Blase and Blase, 2000). From my own experiences, I have worked within settings where I felt that I was listened to and others where I felt that I was silenced. Largely these feelings were due to the leadership within the setting and their attitude towards teacher voice. This impact of school culture on teacher identity and voice will be discussed later in this chapter.

Outside of social media, where and how can teachers express their voice? I have found an outlet for my voice through research, as have others (Smiles and Short, 2006). The range of higher degrees or national professional qualifications on offer means that there are courses available for many different interests – although the cost of self-funding is a financial burden which many may not be able to make, so this is not going to be an appropriate method for all teachers. Instead, research has highlighted how social gatherings for teachers may be positive for teachers in allowing them to develop their voice and have it heard (Kooy, 2006; Sadeghi, 2014). Turning to Twitter again, there is a rise in so-called 'teach meets' – such as #BrewEd – where the focus is less on having an online debate and more on allowing face-to-face contact. This removes the concerns of an online history (which could potentially be used against a member of staff) and also supports teachers in developing relationships and friendship with those outside of their current setting.

These suggestions, added to the growth of blogs (Stitzlein and Quinn, 2012), social media and the use of research in the classroom (Gough, 1994), may well be the way forward for teachers to have their voice heard. However, more research will need to be conducted to understand the impact of such methods on teachers' voices being heard at local and national levels, as well as the effect of grassroots movements on professional lives. What is important to understand is how our identity as teachers impacts upon our lives in the classroom.

Teacher identity

It is my belief that teachers who use their whole life experience make good teachers (Palmer, 2003) and this must therefore include our personal beliefs and values, as these are integral parts of our own personal experience (Goodson, 1991). If the values we live our lives by are part of our personal identity (Hitlin, 2003), it is logical to assume that, as dwellers in our own minds, we take them wherever we go – we cannot take them off and leave them at will. This notion of belief is an essential part of a teacher's transportable identity; it is who they authentically are. This type of teacher is therefore one who is able to maintain these personal values within the professional remit of being a teacher without feeling that they have to become someone else the moment they step over the threshold of a school. It is about being our authentic selves at work as much as we are when we are alone.

During the course of my own thesis research I allowed myself to be my authentic self, to drop the notion of needing to 'be' a researcher or 'be' a specific kind of super-teacher. I simply allowed myself to be the teacher that I already was, gradually understanding that the role of teacher was an intrinsic part of my identity and something which I felt to be more of a vocation than a profession (Schwarz, 1999). Although I welcomed the recognition from others in my school through lesson observations or general comments, I *knew* that I was a good teacher. This experience was born of the fact that I was in a career I was successful in because it was a good fit for *who I already* was. I had not radically changed myself in order to become a teacher. Instead, I had found a career which already fitted my existing personality, beliefs and values.

If we believe that good teachers are simply being who they authentically are (Palmer, 1997) and are called to the classroom through a sense of personal vocation, then this adds weight to the notion of the transportability of beliefs. Good teachers can be made through adequate support of their whole identity – both personal and professional – by respecting the fact that their identity is transportable between home and school. If we neglect the teacher as a whole and real person and begin to see them only as a facilitator of imparting knowledge and skills, then we run the risk of losing the soul of the education system.

Our identities as teachers are not something we put on like a jumper when we walk into school. Instead out teacher identities are the same as our personal identities as we carry and transport them around with us. This idea of a *transportable identity* was based on research by Maynard and Zimmerman (1984). Their original concept limited the transportable parts of our identities to three features: age, sex, and race (Mieroop, 2010). This is possibly because these things are relatively easy to assign

(Nakamura, 2012). However, I believe that there is a deeper level to our transportable identity – more elusive but nonetheless part of ourselves – that we carry from social situation to social situation: our epistemological belief system or our understanding of how we conceptualise and view the knowledge we have. This knowledge includes our beliefs on philosophy, faith, how the world works, what it means to be a human, and everything in between. Research has identified strong links between these beliefs, teachers, and their pupils (Schommer-Aikins, 2004). Deeply held epistemological beliefs are ingrained in who we are. They journey with us wherever we go, including from home to classroom. The 'you' that is in the classroom is the same 'you' that goes everywhere else.

This understanding of an epistemological belief system becomes crucial when teachers face challenging or emotional events in the classroom which in turn lead to deeper relationships. There are times when outside circumstances affect our view and interpretation of the pupils in our care. One cannot help but be personally affected by knowing events that have happened in our pupils' lives: a pupil being taken into local authority care; the death of a close family member; being bullied by their peers.

The role of ethnography

Ethnographic research has strong ties with teacher voice because it is based upon the premise that the researcher is living the experiences they are writing about. Encouraging teachers to think in a more ethnographic way is not about assuming that every one of them is suddenly going to embark on a further degree or qualification. Whether they realise it or not, all teachers are engaged in research on a daily basis. Think about your own daily practice within your setting. You might trial a new way of delivering a topic and then reflect upon how effective it was and if it was successful with your learners. You might rearrange the seating plan of your classroom and then chat with the teacher in the class next door about the impact it had. These simple acts – ones that teachers do on a daily basis without thinking about it – are the basis of ethnographic research in the classroom.

Ethnography can be a means of making invisible school experiences visible. If teachers are able to share with a wider audience more of the experiences they have, then there are fewer dark corners for negative practices and experiences to hide. The sharing of our school lives does not have to be solely through the means of academic research, articles, and books. It is also about teachers meeting and engaging with other teachers in order to discuss their practice and learn from each other. Within the Japanese school system there exists a practice called *jugyou kenkyu*, which can be roughly translated as 'collaborative research on teaching' (Matoba and Sarkar Arani, 2006). This views classroom teaching and school experiences not only as the daily work of teachers, but also as a means of their own development. In Japanese schools, this is a highly structured approach but the principles are adaptable to our own settings. This could be as simple as a department research project on a new way to deliver an element of the curriculum, or a whole-school approach to teaching and learning.

Think about the CPD you might have had over the past two years. There are some brilliant trainers and courses out there, but how often did you sit and wonder what relevance it had to you or question the nature of the claims made? If some of your CPD time was given to you to be able to conduct research directly related to your class/setting/age group, would it have a greater impact on your teaching and ultimately pupil performance? I would argue that it would because ethnographic research encourages you to understand the specific social world you teach within, and that is naturally different in your school than it is in the one down the road. Ethnography values the lived experiences of teachers within the classroom. It places importance on the uniqueness of not only our schools but our individual classrooms too. We have such rich diversity in our education system and we should celebrate and learn from that.

As a profession, we should not feel that research is something beyond us or only for academics. Whilst I understand and value the significance of research conducted by people who are outside our classroom world, I also believe that there is an important place for research conducted by teachers to provide a unique perspective from those who are inside our schools. This is where ethnography becomes so important as it is a means of sharing that rich insider knowledge with an audience that otherwise might have no way of experiencing it themselves.

Bibliography

Anon (2017) *The secret teacher: dispatches from the classroom.* London: Guardian Faber Publishing.

Alamri, N. (2015) 'Teacher voice in curriculum development in Saudi schools', *Proceedings of the 15th International Academic Conference.* Rome, 14th–17th April. Prague: International Institute of Social and Economic Sciences, p. 73.

Barber, M. and Graham, D. (eds) (2013) *Sense and nonsense and the national curriculum.* Abingdon: Routledge.

Blase, J. and Blase, J. (2000) 'Effective instructional leadership: teachers' perspectives on how principals promote teaching and learning in schools', *Journal of Educational Administration* 38 (2) pp. 130–141.

Bragg, S. (2007) '"But I listen to children anyway!" – Teacher perspectives on pupil voice', *Educational Action Research* 15 (4) pp. 505–518.

Brindley, S. (2015) *A critical investigation of the role of teacher research and its relationship to teacher professionalism, knowledge and identity.* PhD thesis. UCL Institute of Education.

Burke, R. J. and Cooper, C. L. (2013) *Voice and whistleblowing in organizations: overcoming fear, fostering courage and unleashing candour.* Cheltenham: Edward Elgar Publishing.

Dana, N. F. (1995) 'Action research, school change, and the silencing of teacher voice', *Action in Teacher Education* 16 (4) pp. 59–70.

Elbaz, F. (1991) 'Research on teacher's knowledge: the evolution of a discourse', *Journal of Curriculum Studies* 23 (1) pp. 1–19.

Goodson, I. F. (1991) 'Sponsoring the teacher's voice: teachers' lives and teacher development', *Cambridge Journal of Education* 21 (1) pp. 35–45.

Goodson, I. F. and Numan, U. (2002) 'Teacher's life worlds, agency and policy contexts', *Teachers and Teaching* 8 (3) pp. 269–277.

Gough, N. (1994) 'Narration, reflection, diffraction: aspects of fiction in educational inquiry', *Australian Educational Researcher* 21 (3) pp. 47–76.

Hargreaves, A. and Shirley, D. (2012) *The far side of educational reform.* Ottawa, ON: Canadian Teachers' Federation.

Hitlin, S. (2003) 'Values as the core of personal identity: drawing links between two theories of self', *Social Psychology Quarterly* 66 (2) pp. 118–137.

Kooy, M. (2006) 'The telling stories of novice teachers: constructing teacher knowledge in book clubs', *Teaching and Teacher Education* 22 (6) pp. 661–674.

Lincoln, Y. S. (1995) 'In search of students' voices', *Theory Into Practice* 34 (2) pp. 88–93.

Matoba, M. and Sarkar Arani, M. R. (2006) 'Ethnography for teachers' professional development: Japanese approach of investigation on classroom activities' in Popov, N., Wolhuter, C., Heller, C. and Kysilka, M. (eds) *Comparative education in teacher training.* Vol. 4. Sofia: Bulgarian Comparative Education Society, pp. 116–125.

Maynard, D. W. and Zimmerman, D. H. (1984) 'Topical talk, ritual and the social organization of relationships', *Social Psychology Quarterly* 47 (4) pp. 301–316.

McIntyre, D., Pedder, D. and Rudduck, J. (2005) 'Pupil voice: comfortable and uncomfortable learnings for teachers', *Research Papers in Education* 20 (2) pp. 149–168.

Nakamura, I. (2012) 'Reflections on learning from a study leave: one year later', *大学教育研究紀要 (Bulletin of Higher Education)* 8, pp. 151–162.

Palmer, P. J. (1997) 'The heart of a teacher identity and integrity in teaching', *Change: The Magazine of Higher Learning* 29 (6) pp. 14–21.

Palmer, P. J. (2003) 'Teaching with heart and soul: reflections on spirituality in teacher education', *Journal of Teacher Education* 54 (5) pp. 376–385.

Papandrea, M.-R. (2012) 'Social media, public school, teachers, and the first amendment', *North Carolina Law Review* 90 (5) pp. 1597–1642.

Reese, W. J. (2002) *Power and the promise of school reform: grassroots movements during the progressive era*. New York, NY: Teachers College Press.

Sadeghi, M. (2014) *Claiming teacher voice through personal narratives: exploring teacher and student agency for learning in classrooms*. Master's thesis. University of Toronto.

Schommer-Aikins, M. (2004) 'Explaining the epistemological belief system: introducing the embedded systemic model and coordinated research approach', *Educational Psychologist* 39 (1) pp. 19–29.

Schwarz, G. E. (1999) 'Teaching as vocation: enabling ethical practice', *The Educational Forum* 63 (1) pp. 23–29.

Smiles, T. L. and Short, K. G. (2006) 'Transforming teacher voice through writing for publication', *Teacher Education Quarterly* 33 (3) pp. 133–147.

Stitzlein, S. M. and Quinn, S. (2012) 'What can we learn from teacher dissent online?', *The Educational Forum* 76 (2) pp. 190–200.

Van De Mieroop, D. (2010) 'Making transportable identities relevant as a persuasive device: the case of Hillary Clinton's 2008 concession speech', *Hermes – Journal of Language and Communication Studies* 23 (44) pp. 229–239.

Reflections

Chapter 12 - Conclusions

Teaching is a wonderful job. It is a privilege to spend so much time with learners at such a crucial stage in their lives. However, it is also a challenging and demanding job, one in which we all experience times of stress. The difference for teachers in toxic schools is that those difficult times appear to have no end, with many seeing their only option as leaving.

Immersing ourselves in the world of the classroom – and the experiences of those who work in them – is crucial in understanding not only what effective teaching is for learners but also what kind of work environment is best for staff to teach within. The only way we can achieve this is by hearing the authentic voices of teachers who experience that world on a daily basis, taking what they have to say seriously. Many teachers will enjoy a happy, healthy and fulfilling career. Recently, a former headteacher of mine passed away. His career spanned several decades, including over 20 years at the school I attended. His funeral was a celebration of a life in education in a career he remained passionate about. Hearing these positive messages about education and teaching is crucial but we should not shy away from shining a light into the darker side of our schools; it is only when the light is shined into the darkness that we can truly begin to banish it.

The aim of *Toxic Schools* has been to highlight the impact that negative teaching experiences can have, both on careers and on the health and wellbeing of staff. It is important to acknowledge the fact that there are colleagues struggling on a daily basis because of the teaching environment they work within; we cannot turn away and simply hope that it does not happen to us. We are all in this together. As a profession, we have the capacity to change the culture of our schools from within. Whilst we all acknowledge that there are pressures outside of our control, how we treat each other, how we support and develop staff, how we handle challenging situations – these are all down to us. We should aim to keep the experienced staff we have whilst nurturing those at the start of their career. If a teacher wants it, teaching should be a lifelong career where they too can retire after a life of service to others, as my former headteacher did. Yet for many this is not the case.

Under our current education system, we are losing teachers each year who simply feel that they have no other choice but to leave a job they used to love, a job they were good at, a job where they were in a position to change the lives of the learners in their classroom. Teaching should not be what it has become for many: the survival of the fittest. As a profession, we should not feel proud that we have 'coped'; none of us should be made to feel that coping is the only strategy we have. As a profession, we should not allow good teachers to have their own health and wellbeing damaged simply by turning up to work. Teaching is our profession and we should not feel under any criticism from others for wanting the best for those working within it.

If you are working in a difficult situation, it can be useful to consider your values and how they are measured. Do they lie in or out of your control? As a teacher, I've written and have reflected on my vision and values for three decades. On the whole, they have been tweaked but have never changed fundamentally. I suspect they mirror your own as an educator:

- First and foremost, schools must have structures in place to ensure that all students are safe so that teachers are able to teach as freely as possible within a flexible timetable and curriculum, to enrich students, and to contribute fully to school life.
- Secondly, it is important to make learning challenging and as relevant as possible for all students, including the most disaffected.
- Finally, schools must equip students to leave school with a portfolio of qualifications, teaching students character and resilience so that they can contribute to the wider society in their adult lives.

I suspect these are values we all share, but how these values are evaluated at a whole-school level is another matter. And what metrics do we use? Which of the above are in my control and which come under collective teacher efficacy? Ultimately, we all contribute to the success of a school.

There is a subtle difference here between managing our expectations and success.

We appear to have a structure within the English system where anyone and everyone can now fall victim to our accountability processes in the teaching profession. Long gone are the days where a very poor teacher would be isolated and it would require a lengthy procedure to remove somebody from the classroom. Teachers are now regularly voting with their feet and schools are genuinely struggling to recruit. Today, you may only have one candidate for an advertised job instead of 10 or 50 applicants.

In 2017, we lost more teachers from the profession than we gained from those entering it – for the first time in the history of school census data-collection. The prevalence of mental health problems in teachers, social media incidents and student exclusions has never been higher. And we do not appear to be funding schools sufficiently well to create the 'world-class education system' desired by our politicians.

Every few years, we pass from one from government to the next and receive new statutory policies and buzzwords, plus new measures of effectiveness – all of which fail to recognise that what we've tried in the past hasn't worked. As I write, Ofsted are planning to release a new school inspection framework in September 2019 that will take a broader view on 'outcomes' and focus closely on how schools are offering a curriculum in the broadest sense.

It baffles me that the people in positions of power who are there for a good reason are paid to take on this great responsibility, yet fail to recognise problems or take any bold action that might actually make a difference. For example: stripping back the accountability processes that have created the problems in the first place.

Measure a school by its ability to grow apple trees and every school will plant apple seeds. Judge schools by their examination outcomes – regardless of demographic context – and schools will do anything and everything to squeeze a performance out of their students. Some schools (and some students) will win and some will lose.

I accept that teachers are more immersed in research and cognitive science than they were several years ago, but what teachers actually do in the classroom remains largely the same. We still get paid on a shoestring; work excessive hours; teach large classes and on the whole teach effectively, year in, year out.

We have created an education system where we accept that teachers – good teachers – would rather jump ship than work 60- to 80-hour weeks to keep up with the paperwork – evidence trials, data collection, marking and lesson planning. This paperwork is often required, sometimes demanded, weeks in advance or with less than 24 hours' notice – which doesn't seem to be in balance with the 20 or so hours of contact time in the classroom each week. Teachers are now expert form-fillers rather than masters of their classrooms.

However, there is a way we can achieve common sense in our profession – and I do hope the Secretary of State for Education takes note.

In the past 12 months, one of the most fascinating opportunities presented to me was to sit on the accountability commission group for the National Association of Head Teachers (NAHT) in March to July 2018, developing a new vision for the future of school accountability.

Together we recognised the range and importance of all forms of accountability, including financial oversight and governance, and in particular the role of governing boards and trusts. What wasn't published was the core topic of this book – toxic schools and its drivers.

This terminology aside, the focus was on the current system that was considered to have the greatest negative impact on schools and pupils: the use of performance data and the role of the inspectorate. The current problems were agreed by the group to limit the potential of our education system. It was found that the current accountability system:

- limits ambition.
- incentivises self-interest.
- deters talented staff from working in more deprived communities.
- narrows the curriculum and encourages teaching to the test.
- diverts attention from teaching and learning.
- drives good people from the profession.
- provides less assurance of standards.

In essence, the nine recommendations from the 32-page report highlighted a set of opportunities that were a 'win for all stakeholders':

- Comparative performance data should be used by Ofsted to inform judgements of school effectiveness.
- The Department for Education should use a 'requires improvement' judgement as the trigger for funded support and as a replacement for floor and coasting standards.
- Ofsted should adopt a new role, focused on identifying failure and providing stronger diagnostic insight for schools that are struggling.
- The Department for Education should end the exemption from inspection for previously 'outstanding' schools and commit Ofsted to inspect all schools on a transparent cycle of inspection.
- The 'outstanding' judgement should be replaced with a more robust system for identifying specific excellence within the sector in order to increase the take-up of highly effective, evidence-based practice.
- Ofsted should commission research to determine the format and nature of inspection required to provide reliable judgements and reciprocal benefits for schools.
- Existing peer review programmes should be evaluated to identify characteristics of effective practice in order to develop national accreditation arrangements.
- An invitation should be extended to the Chartered College of Teaching, through the Leadership Development Advisory Group, to produce alternative national standards for headteachers that better reflect the professional behaviours, practice and knowledge required for achieving excellence.
- The Department for Education should extend the career progression strategy to support recently appointed headteachers in the critical first years of headship.

If the Department for Education truly wanted to strip back the accountability and stop good teachers leaving the profession, reduce the number of mental health issues in our schools, and control extortionate CEO salaries, then they would start implementing many of these recommendations and seek to build in future sustainability for all governments.

The necessary movement would come from leadership at the very top and the trust required for us to get on with the job in hand. The fact of the matter is that I do not believe our politicians want this change or have any firm grasp of the issues or how to resolve them. At least with the College of Teaching, there is some hope to flip the toxic culture in favour of educating our young people – away from flawed league table methodology and the marketisation of a profession that is starting to see the impact of recent reforms disguised as granting greater autonomy. If we want true autonomy, then we must revert back to working together, rather than against one another – only then can we eradicate the toxic behaviours that are rapidly appearing in our classrooms, corridors and line-management conversations.

If you are feeling the strain, you are not alone. Helen and I have both been there. Get in touch with either of us and, in good faith, we will point you in the direction of some professional support. Oh, and now you've finished this book, leave it on the desk of someone you know needs to evaluate their behaviour.

Reflections

Index

D

E

F

G

H

I

L

M

N

O

P

R

S

T

V

W

List of abbreviations

ASCL Association of School and College Leaders

BA Bachelor of Arts

BEd Bachelor of Education

CAMHS Child Adolescent & Mental Health Service

CPD Continuing Professional Development

EYFS Early Years Foundation Stage

GTU Graduate Teacher Programme

HLTAs Higher Level Teaching Assistants

HND Higher National Diploma

IT Information Technology

ITT Initial Teacher Training

LSA Learning Support Assistant

MAT Multi-Academy Trust

MLT Middle Leadership Team

MPS Main Pay Scale

NFER National Foundation for Educational Research

NPQML National Professional Qualification for Middle Leadership

NQT Newly Qualified Teacher

OECD Organisation for Economic Co-operation and Development

ONS Office of National Statistics

PE Physical Education

PGCE Postgraduate Certificate in Education

PLMD Profound and multiple learning disabilities

PRU Pupil Referral Unit

PTSD Post-traumatic stress disorder

PTA Parent-Teacher Association

SATs Standard Assessment Tests

SEN Special Educational Needs

SEND Special Educational Needs and Disability

SLT Senior Leadership Team

TA Teaching Assistant